FATHER'S DAYS

FATHER'S DAYS

A True Story of Incest

KATHERINE BRADY

Seaview Books
New York

Designed by Tere LoPrete

Library of Congress Cataloging in Publication Data

Brady, Katherine.
    Father's days.

    1. Incest. 2. Brady, Katherine. I. Title.
HQ71.B68   301.41'58   79-4878
ISBN 0-87223-539-4

For the two most important people in my life—my daughters

Foreword

Gazing from my window high up in a New York City apartment building, I'm astonished by what I see, amazed to find myself here. Three years ago, looking out another window, I saw land stretching before me, part of it covered with green grass, smooth and flawless as a rug, part with graceful spruce trees and beautiful wild growth, all ending at the slender blue thread of the Ogemaw River, which bisects Great Rapids, Minnesota. It's ironic that I'm freer here in four small rooms, surrounded by the urban crush, than I was in the twelve open, airy rooms of that house by the river.

The journey between these places happened in a short time. But how long it was—as long as a lifetime. It took me back to places I'd never wanted to go again. I felt things I'd hoped were buried forever. I was not always a willing traveler; it was an agonizing, arduous trip. But it gave me back my life, which I hadn't possessed for nearly thirty years, and so I cannot regret a single moment of it.

Three years ago, when I was thirty-two years old, I didn't really understand what the word "incest" meant, although

I had had a sexual relationship with my father that lasted ten years. Three years ago I thought I was the only person who'd ever had such an experience. I believed this was something that had happened in the past and remained there, unfortunate but finished.

As I've unraveled the legacy of my childhood these last few years I've learned that incest is alarmingly common. I've learned that my entire life was shaped by its happening to me. And I've learned that by looking at it—releasing it from the prison of the past, letting it rise up into the present—I could at last leave it behind.

FATHER'S DAYS

CHAPTER

1

"You've got to put the past to rest. Nothing will ever be gained by reliving it day to day. But it is so hard to overcome."

—*Ellen*

My memory begins in 1948, my fourth year, with my older sister, Ellen, and I crouched down in the small stand of scraggly trees near our trailer, peering out at Mother as she tried to teach herself to ride Dad's bike. She sputtered and swore and fell regularly. We worked hard to suppress our giggles, knowing if she caught us we'd be severely scolded. We seemed to get on her nerves anyway; she'd be even more annoyed if she discovered we were spying on her.

It would have been difficult *not* to notice her. No privacy was available in or around the trailer. A squat gray structure with a white roof, the Quonset hut which served as my parents' bedroom protruding from one side, it was a distinct oddity on a street of small frame houses. When we'd arrived in Hartland, Minnesota, for my father to assume his position as a guard at Minnesota Central State Prison, a repository for criminals deemed beyond rehabilitation, my parents had been unable to find a house to rent and bought the trailer instead. Its two dark rooms were sparsely furnished, the only color provided by wildly flowered curtains in the three small windows. At night two narrow beds were pulled out from beneath the kitchen cupboards for Ellen and me.

Mother was pregnant, and her disposition worsened with each passing month. Ellen and I were too noisy, she said, and she often screamed at us to keep quiet, to play outside where she couldn't hear us. I tried to stay out of her way, running about in the hot, unshaded yard with my dog, wandering down the street to visit my best friend, Ruthie, despite the fact that her parents were perpetually grumpy and didn't enjoy having children around either.

But apparently Ellen and I didn't give Mother a wide enough berth. That summer, when she was in her eighth month, we were sent to stay with relatives, I with Grandma Hinkle, my mother's mother, Ellen with Aunt Flora, my father's sister.

I was bereft, so desperately homesick for my mother that I wailed and whined until my grandparents capitulated and called Mother on the phone so that I could hear her voice. I didn't miss my father at all. He was rather a vague figure to me, the man who hadn't seen me until I was two years old and paid little attention to me even then. The story went that he doted on Ellen, the pretty and immaculate little girl he'd known before going off to fight in the war, and had no idea what to do with me, a grubby, demanding, and strange two-year-old. I was an annoyance to him, an irritant. The only pleasant contact between us was when he'd hold me on his lap at night and rock me to sleep.

After talking to my mother on the phone I was sufficiently pacified to enjoy being the center of my grandparents' attention. Despite an arduous work schedule, Grandma Hinkle demonstrated amply that she cared very much for me—a homemade cruller in the middle of the afternoon, special rhymes she chanted only for me, frequent enveloping embraces. And the farm itself was a magical place. I loved being awakened by the rooster's crowing and looking down from my bedroom window into the trees of the orchard, heavy with blossoms, fruit, and songbirds. I loved Blackie, the diminutive Shetland pony, and the fierce bull that I teased with a shred of red cloth, ignoring Grandpa's admonition not to. I contented myself for hours by hanging on to the end of a long rope suspended from the ceiling of the barn, swinging in an ever-widening arc and releasing myself, flying into the haymow, tumbling happily in the loose straw—which was also off limits. And I loved to go along with him at the end of the day into the pastures where he and one of the farm dogs herded the cows back toward the barn for milking. On these journeys the terrible homesickness, my loneliness for Mother, came over me in great, wrenching waves. I cried for her at the end of every day.

But my return home in August, a few days after my brother, Andrew, was born, wasn't at all as I'd imagined it lying in my bed at Grandma's. Mother couldn't bear to have Ellen or me touch her. She was crankier than she'd been before we went away, and she seemed to spend all her time fussing over the baby.

Ellen and I crept into Mother and Dad's bedroom one day, then stuck our heads around the corner to peer at Mother while she changed Andy's diapers on the kitchen counter. Sensing our presence, she whirled angrily in our direction.

"Don't bother me," she snapped. "Can't you see I'm busy with the baby?"

Ellen stuck out her tongue. Mother poked hers out at Ellen. Ellen muttered something nasty, and we were confined to the bedroom for the afternoon. I was hurt by this punishment; it made Ellen angry. The responses were typical of each of us throughout our childhod.

Ellen had possessed most-favored status in the family before Andrew was born. By the time we returned from our exiles that summer of his birth, she had clearly been supplanted in that regard by the new and adored baby boy. This was a terrible blow to her, and she responded by developing a mysterious illness at least once a year during the rest of her grade-school career.

In the winter of 1949 we moved from the cramped trailer to a rambling old Victorian farmhouse surrounded by three acres of land in the country outside of Hartland. It had drawbacks: the general disrepair and filth from years of neglect by the previous owner, the dirt floor in the kitchen, the musty smell that pervaded the rooms. But it also had space, inside and out—a creek that ran alongside the driveway; a huge old barn that still contained horses' harnesses, hanging ghostlike from wooden pegs on the walls, stacks of ancient magazines, and the faint odor of chickens who'd lived there years before; and several sheds scattered around the property.

The upstairs rooms were too dilapidated to use initially, so Ellen and I slept downstairs in what would eventually become the living room, while Andy slept in an alcove off my parents' bedroom, also on the ground floor. Ellen and

I slept on Army cots, painted Army green, and gazed up at a flaking ceiling, surrounded by walls whose paper was stained and occasionally peeling around the edges. But at least we had our own room. Mother was nearby and less tense than she had been, her irritableness now identified as having been caused by "a breakdown." Dad was strict, and often remote, but very handsome and still willing to hold me on his lap along with Andy. And we were all together, which made me very happy.

Mother escorted me to my first day of school in the fall of 1949, leading me across the playground, holding my hand, taking me inside, and staying with me for a few minutes. I liked school immediately, especially enjoying finger painting with bright colors on large sheets of paper and listening to my teacher play the piano or read stories. The only thing I didn't like was running into Ellen on the playground.

"You're such a dirty little thing," she'd say, accurately describing me, shooing me away from her. "Go on. You're too grubby to play with."

"Poor little Kathy," the other kids would chant in sing-song voices. "Her sister doesn't want to play with her."

And I felt like "poor little Kathy." Not angered by Ellen's treatment of me, not indignant, just hurt. She was beginning her rejection of familial things, and I was her first, most convenient target.

It's true that I presented a rather grimy appearance. I think I began the day most often dressed in clean clothes, usually hand-me-downs we received by the bagful from people at the church, always blue jeans, a shirt or sweater, and my corrective shoes, which laced up nearly to the knees. But I played outdoors and I played hard; it didn't take long for me to look quite gray around the edges. I didn't really care, and Mother couldn't, or didn't bother to, keep up with me.

At home Ellen and I were forced to spend time together. From the time I was six and she was eight, the housecleaning chores were turned over to us each Saturday. Mother despised housework and happily put us in charge of it while she and Dad went into town to shop, taking Andy with them. Ellen resented this terribly and was particularly surly on Saturdays, when she was most aware of the injustice of it all. We fought over what radio program we'd listen to while we worked (I liked Arthur Godfrey, whom she hated because Mother liked him), what tasks each of us would perform, our opinions of Mother. She called me "Mama's baby," spitting the epithet at me with contempt.

And I was. Still desperately needing Mother's attention, suffering acutely from her absence each summer during stays with relatives, I cherished the time I spent with her. I loved Saturday night, bath night, washing in the big iron tub set in the center of the kitchen, Mother soaping my body and rinsing it off. I liked also to be sick, because she would minister to me, her training as a nurse coming to the fore, her competent hands pressing cold cloths against my forehead. I stationed myself in the kitchen to watch her early on Saturday mornings, when she'd bake upside-down butterscotch biscuits that filled the entire house with their delicious aroma. I liked accompanying her to church before my Sunday school class, sitting beside her in the old oak pew, staring at the flickering candles, in which I sometimes thought I could see the face of Jesus. I loved recounting to myself and others the story of her heroism during the tornado of August, 1950: how she saw it coming and herded her children into the underground fruit cellar, slamming the doors over our heads just moments before the wind raced by, uprooting huge trees, flattening the old barn. She was afraid; I could feel her fear. But she acted decisively and kept us safe. Nevertheless, I carried from that time on a great fear of wind.

With the lumber from the old barn, Dad began building a new barn, a garage, and a breezeway that would run between the garage and the house. Like any project he undertook, this became a subject for argument between him and Mother. He worked very slowly, doing everything himself, the quintessential loner without buddies to call on for assistance. The only activity he ever undertook with other people was hunting, something he did often with other men from work.

This was another sore spot with Mother. He never consulted with her ahead of time. He just announced he was going. This invariably caused her to hark back to the time when he'd joined the Marines and gone off to war. He hadn't asked her opinion; he'd presented her with a *fait accompli*. She was pregnant with me at the time, and she never forgave him.

"He deserted me," she always said.

His hunting trips were reminders of the old wound. She also resented that he managed somehow, no matter the state of family finances, to be splendidly outfitted for these excursions: new gun, proper clothing, expensive boots, ample ammunition, and traveling money in his pocket.

At the same time that Dad began building the new barn, he erected a playhouse for us. It stood between the huge field where we grew sweet corn to sell to market and the vegetable garden that we cultivated for ourselves. I spent hours in the playhouse, conversing with an imaginary friend, playing house, giving dramatic presentations. Occasionally Ellen or Andy would join me, but most of the time there I spent alone. Ellen preferred to be in the house; Andy liked to hang around the barn, particularly by the large barrel in front of it where Dad burned the trash each day. Andy was fascinated by the fire always smoldering inside it.

I liked playing with real children, too, and there were plenty of them around. Across the highway were the five Dykema kids, wild and somewhat unruly, whose mother looked like Dale Evans until she had a nervous collapse and aged years in the months she was institutionalized. Beyond the creek lived Betty and Billy Schwimmer, the first kids I knew to have a television set, at whose house I watched and learned to love Howdy Doody. On the far side of the cornfield were Susan and Johnny Mueller, children of the prison warden, who kept his lawn carefully manicured and weed-free through the assistance of one or another of the honor inmates who were always in residence over the garage. I found these men rather frightening and the Mueller house itself oppressive in its formality and the number of rules one had to obey when inside it.

Not that I wasn't used to rules and obedience. Dad insisted on both. He enacted the part of stern law enforcer at home as well as at work. His regulations were stringent. If he sensed an infringement, his interrogation was relentless. His punishments were harsh. Mother objected to his strictness and his methods, but he never took her protests seriously. He was over six feet tall, well built, domineering; she was just five feet tall, slight, a sputterer. He could silence her with a glance.

Once he noticed some small change missing from his pants pocket. At dinner that night, he dropped a handful of coins onto the table and gazed accusingly at each of us.

"All right," he growled, "who took it?"

Silence.

"Don't you know stealing is against the law? Who took it?"

Continued silence.

"Those men at the prison are crooks and thieves, and that's just what you'll become if you don't understand that stealing is a crime. Now you're all going to sit here until someone confesses."

"Oh, Tom . . ." Mother began to protest.

"You be quiet, Lou." He cut her off. "I'll take care of this."

I knew Ellen had taken the money. I'd often seen her dip her hand into Dad's pocket when his pants were hanging on the bathroom doorknob. I also knew she was guilty by looking at the rebellious grin on her face. But neither of us said anything. Andy had no idea what was going on.

We sat at the table for a very long time that night, listening to Dad's continuing lecture on the law, the Ten Commandments, our future lives as crooks, our need to learn lessons. Finally, when no one broke, he announced we were all confined to the house for a week, except for school. Television privileges were revoked, and we were to receive no treats for a month. There went the five-cent ice cream cones or bottles of soda we had on Friday nights when we drove into Hartland and sat in the car on Main Street watching the passersby, one of the main forms of family entertainment in those days.

Ellen never gave an inch in any of these confrontations.

She met Dad's accusations with silence or a snicker. To Mother she always talked back, in vivid language, completely undaunted by the broad end of the laundry stick which Mother swung in her direction, seemingly unafraid of anything either parent could deal out to her. The only times she was not openly defiant were when she suffered from the strange malaise which afflicted her each spring, keeping her out of school.

Mother responded to this evident plea for help and attention and endorsed the school principal's suggestion that Ellen see a special counselor. Dad dismissed the idea out of hand, enraged at the school's sticking its nose into his family's business, maintaining that the fault was all Mother's anyway.

"You pick on that girl every minute, Lou," he said. "You never give her a minute's peace."

But despite the dissatisfactions and tensions of our household, I was content as long as we were together. Summers away from my family were agonizing, July and August of 1951 being especially bleak.

I spent that time with Mother's oldest brother, Peter, and his wife, Aunt Winifred. I helped out as much as I could with their three young boys—changing diapers, assisting them at feeding time, playing with them in the yard in front of the farmhouse—but I was only seven, and still felt very much like a baby myself. I longed for the kind of attention the boys were receiving. I wanted to be able to tell my aunt how desolate I felt, to have her hold and comfort me, but I could never find the words and she remained quite distant. Uncle Peter didn't want me underfoot while he and his men were doing farm chores, so I tended to avoid him also.

The one bright spot of my visit was learning to ride the farm pony bareback. When Mother and Dad came to pick me up on a hot August morning, I ran to the stable to get out the pony, led her to a conspicuous spot, and prepared to show them my expertise. Moving several yards away from the tiny horse, I headed for her on the run, leaped into the air as I approached, and sailed right over her back, landing on the ground on the opposite side with a heavy thud. They applauded me anyway, and I landed in the right spot on the second try.

During the time we were away that summer, the front room that had been Ellen's and my bedroom had been done over, its walls covered with knotty pine, a small black-and-white television placed on a low table, a sofa and two large armchairs where the Army cots had been, large floral-print curtains bordering the windows, still-life prints in maple frames hanging on the walls. Ellen and I had been moved to the second story, a distant and barren territory. I'd liked being downstairs, close to Mother and Dad. I'd felt secure knowing they were nearby. Ellen hated the idea that we had to continue sharing a room. She didn't like having me around, and was most eager now for maximum privacy.

The only good thing about being upstairs was my proximity to the spare room down the hall. It was used exclusively for storage, and I was fascinated by the contents of the boxes piled inside it. Most interesting were my father's war mementos: a Japanese parachute whose strong silk string was perfect for the practice of home dentistry with one end tied around a doorknob and the other attached to a wobbly tooth; a long sword that gleamed like silver when it was unsheathed; a Japanese officer's uniform, including helmet; and a pair of silk kimonos, one blood red, one rich royal blue, both emblazoned with golden dragons.

Along with these talismans of the past there was also a bed in the room, and when I was almost eight, I found myself often crawling beneath its blankets, exploring my body's covert and mysterious places with the aid of a mirror and flashlight, moving as little as possible so the bed wouldn't squeak and alert anyone to my presence in the room.

I thought what I saw in the mirror was ugly, but my exploring fingers produced an enjoyable sensation. Pursuing this, letting mirror and flashlight drop, I found that the harder I rubbed, the more intense the sensation became, the warmer my body grew. And one day, after these feelings rose to an acute pitch, something else happened. I didn't know what it was, this explosive flush that radiated out from the center of my body, but I knew that it was pleasurable, that I liked feeling it, and that it was undoubtedly wrong, a sin. I also knew instinctively that it was a secret I must carefully guard.

Late in the autumn of 1951, having just indulged in this nameless sin in the spare room, I was moving very quietly down the stairs and toward the kitchen when I heard Mother talking to someone. It was unusual for her to have a friend at the house, and I stopped to hear what they were saying.

"Sometimes I think I'm going to pop," Mother said.

"Probably the housework is getting you down." The voice belonged to Harriet Williams, Mother's one true friend and confidante. "You never liked it."

"I think I'm just going to burst."

"Why don't you go back to work, Louise?" Harriet asked.

"Tom would have a fit!" Mother shrieked. "You know the way he thinks—women belong at home and they should stay at home."

"Well," said Harriet, "is it better to stay home and resent it and let the kids drive you crazy?"

"I'd have a real fight on my hands to talk him into letting me go to work."

"So? Maybe you have to think of what's going to be best in the long run."

"I know you're right, Harriet." Mother's tone was hesitant despite her words. "If I worked, at least we'd have a little more money and I'd have some peace of mind."

And she began to plead her case with Dad. She didn't mention that we got on her nerves; she didn't say how much she hated housework. She based her argument on financial need. We lived from paycheck to paycheck. If she worked, we could add a few extras to the monthly budget, stop wearing secondhand clothes from the church, do some more work on the house, perhaps even have something left over at the end of the month.

Dad didn't buy it. He felt her primary motive was a desire to get away from the house, to get out on her own. He pointed out all the improvements in the house we'd made on his salary: the new floor in the kitchen, the concrete breezeway between the house and the garage, redoing the living room, fixing the upstairs bedroom. We were hardly desperate, he pointed out; he'd rather have her at home.

But Mother was determined. Sometimes she argued with him head-on, vigorously refuting his points, anger making her tiny body resemble a bantam rooster's as she strutted around the kitchen, face reddening, finger jabbing in the air. Sometimes she just sat by in silence while he grumbled, venting his self-pity. And every once in a while she dragged out the favorite weapon in her arsenal: "You deserted me."

"And there I was, all alone in Chicago," she'd say, "one baby already and another on the way, and *you deserted me.*"

Her use of this hardy perennial tended, of course, to confirm Dad's thesis that she just wanted to get away. Her statement implied that turnabout was fair play and she now had a right to desert him. She was owed one.

In the spring of 1952, despite Dad's continuing objections, Mother took a nursing job at Elmhurst Hospital, drawing on the training and work experience she'd had before she was married. She worked the night shift, from 11:00 P.M. to 7:00 A.M., leaving the house about 10:30 for the half-hour drive to the hospital. Dad, at this time, worked the 2:00–10:00 P.M. shift at the prison. My parents felt strongly that their children should never be left alone or with strangers, and they arranged their work schedules so that one of them was always at home with us. The rule, they said, was for our safety.

When Mother began working I felt the same sense of abandonment and loneliness I'd experienced during the summers I'd been shipped off to relatives. I missed her terribly. Even when she was at home she was difficult to reach, usually sleeping most of the day, tired when she awakened, preoccupied with preparing for work during the evening.

I became afraid of the dark and the shadowy shapes that took form in it. Clothing draped over chairs looked like snakes; lying in heaps on the floor, it resembled small animals, crouching, ready to pounce. Often I thought I saw the silhouette of a man hovering near the window.

I also began to dream of death, feeling myself plummeting down a tunnel, the speed squeezing the breath from my body, stars spinning around me as I felt myself cease to breathe. I told Mother of my dreams and my fears, and each night before leaving for work she came into my room and tried to assure me that I was safe.

One night a few months after she began working, a summer storm blew up suddenly, its high winds rattling the whole house and whistling through the slats of the second-story no-man's-land I shared with Ellen. I'd been asleep for a few hours but I awakened abruptly, the sound and movement of the wind frightening me. I could sense that Ellen was still sleeping, and I lay very still, trying to be brave, trying to remember Mother's reassurances a few hours earlier.

The wind moaned around the corner of the house, catching the loose shutter on the spare-room window, banging it against the side of the old frame structure, causing it to shudder. My fear grew, and I slipped my feet over the edge of the bed and braced myself to travel through the dark toward the stairs.

Reaching them, I could see a spill of light from the living-room lamp my parents always left on in case Ellen or I had to use the stairs at night. I hurried down and knocked as loudly as I could on my parents' bedroom door.

"Is that you, Katy?" My father's voice, fuzzy with sleep, reached me in the hallway.

"I'm scared," I whimpered.

"Come in here by me," he called out. "I'll fix you up."

CHAPTER

2

"It takes all kinds of people to keep this old world going. It would be terrible if we were all alike."

—Dad

When I heard my father's voice inviting me into his room, my fear began to vanish. It disappeared altogether when he wrapped one long arm around me as I crawled into bed next to him.

"You don't have to be afraid ever. I'm right here." He patted my back with his large hand, pressed my head onto his shoulder, gently kissed my neck. He slept only in shorts, and I could feel the warmth of his skin through my pajamas. The strength of his arms, the solidity of his long body, comforted me.

He was proud of his physical appearance, and at thirty-nine he was still a fine-looking man, something I'd begun to notice recently. At a gathering of the Crosley family, I saw he was easily the most handsome of the five sons, and I was proud of that. I'd even taken to carrying a picture of him to show my friends. It didn't matter that it was nearly ten years old, from his days as a Marine. It was my favorite. It showed his blond hair tinted a shimmering gold, his cheeks blushed with pink, his lips rosy and smiling slightly, but not enough to show his one physical flaw, two somewhat crooked front teeth.

"You can come in here and sleep with me anytime you get scared, Katy," he said, his voice odd now, different from any I'd ever heard before. It bore no resemblance to the stern tone he used when ordering me to clean up my plate or tidy my room. It was soft, deeper than usual. It seemed to ooze out of him.

"Why does Mother have to work all night?" I asked.

"She doesn't have to." His familiar gruff voice returned. "She just thinks she does. I've told her I don't like her gone at night, but she just does what she wants anyway. She thinks she's smarter than I am because she went to college."

"I don't like it when she's gone," I said softly.

"Maybe what she really wants is to get away from me," he said, the strangeness back in his voice, a goofy-sounding giggle punctuating the end of the line.

I felt uneasy. "I don't like it when you talk about Mother that way," I said, not even knowing what I meant.

"Oh, you be quiet." He pulled me tighter against him. "I'm just fooling."

I squirmed around so that my back was to him. I tugged the covers over me, trying to signal a desire to sleep. I didn't like this new voice of his. I wanted to forget it.

"Remember," he whispered, "you can come in anytime except when your ma's around."

"Why can't I come in then?" I asked.

"She doesn't like to share her bed with other women."
Again that snicker.

My body pulled away from his involuntarily. He drew
me back, his hands rubbing up and down my arms, legs,
back.

"And, Katy," he cooed, "don't say anything to your ma
about us being in bed talking."

I hated the voice, but his hands were soothing.

"Why not, Dad?"

"Because, that's why. Just because."

And I didn't say anything, not on that day nor on any
of the others when I crawled out of my bed in the night
or the early morning and went downstairs to get into his,
letting those big hands rub over me, erasing the insecurity,
the fear. I already had one secret, I reasoned: the thing I
did in the spare room that felt so good and was probably
so awful. I might just as well have two.

The extra attention from Dad made me miss Mother
less. And it wasn't only when he caressed me in bed that
he made me feel special. He began taking me along with
him in the car when he did errands. He called me Sport. He
bought me a rifle and taught me how to shoot. He managed
to get me a membership in the Hartland Rifle Club, the
only girl so honored. He took me squirrel hunting and
promised trips to hunt deer in the future. I learned how to
track, set up camp, pitch a tent using poles made from
freshly stripped trees.

The bickering between my parents escalated. They didn't
see each other often. Mother arrived home in the morning
and went directly to bed. Dad went to work in the afternoon, and when he returned at night she was just leaving.
The time they had together they spent sniping at each
other.

He grumbled about having to take on more chores around the house, although he seemed to enjoy making us kids breakfast and getting us off to school. She complained of being tired. She pushed him incessantly to go to church. He stubbornly refused, impugning her family's strict German Methodism.

"Just because your family's crazy on the subject of religion doesn't mean I have to be," he'd say.

"But, Tom," she'd whine, "we can't raise these kids without formal religion. You have to be an example too."

"You do it," he'd retort. "I do other things."

They quarreled over Ellen's annual spring illness, his unbending clean-plate rule, grocery shopping, the garden. They tended to steer clear of confrontation on the major issue of Mother's working, which she had now dressed up in high-flown altruism.

"As long as I can remember," she'd tell me, "I've wanted to take care of others."

My father, I'm sure, felt Mother's return to work as a negative comment on his ability as a provider and his stature as a mate. It said to him that he was unable to give her either the material goods or the companionship that she needed to be fulfilled. But he never told Mother this. He kept the hurt and resentment to himself.

His staying silent about it was fine with her. She was something of a martyr, preferring to bear a cross and complain about its weight rather than discuss a problem and perhaps solve it and have the cross removed.

When Harriet inquired about Dad's response to her new career, Mother answered, "Oh, you know, I just pretend everything's okay."

Those rare times when *the* subject was actually let out of the bag, the dialogue was always the same.

"You're the one who made me independent when you deserted me and went into the Marines. You made me like this, and now you can't stand it."

"You'll just never forget that, will you? But I had no choice. I was ashamed to stay home."

"I was a clinging vine until you deserted me, and then I had to learn how to take care of myself—and fast!"

"That's over and done with. Can't you forget it? What good does it do to dredge it up now?"

"If you'd really cared for me you would never have gone in the first place."

Mother's absence, Dad's increasing presence, and the tension between the two of them affected both Ellen and me severely. She now called me "Daddy's baby" with just as much scorn as she'd had for my link with Mother years before. She was angrier than ever with Mother, watching her spend newly earned money on snowy-white uniforms while continuing to dress us in clothes from the church, going off to work and leaving us with an even heavier load of household chores. She was also continually angry with Dad. He'd begun bursting in on her when she was in the bathroom or in her bedroom, "just to check," he said. He demanded that she leave the doors open so he could see what she was doing.

Ellen was also disgusted by the suggestive remarks he'd started making to her: "If you need to know anything about stuff like sex, you just ask me." "You've got pretty good-looking legs, you know that?" "You don't need to go to the movies. You'll just get bad ideas." "What's wrong, girl? You got hot pants or something?"

And she resented both my parents for what she saw as their capitulation to Andrew, the easy, undemanding child who got whatever he asked for.

I felt neither anger nor resentment but only loneliness
and hurt, those two staples of my emotional vocabulary.
But obviously I was also very disturbed by matters at home.
When I entered third grade in the fall of 1952, I began to
steal from my teacher. She kept her purse in a closet near
the back of the room, and occasionally the closet door was
left ajar and the purse itself unclasped. When these conditions prevailed, I quickly reached out as I passed by, darted
my hand into her purse, and extracted whatever change I
could in one fast grab. I always spent the money that
afternoon, at a candy store on the way home from school.
Occasionally, while I was buying Twinkies or a Milky Way,
my favorites, I stole other candy as well. The stealing made
me feel very guilty, but I continued to do it throughout
the year.

I did something else quite uncharacteristic that year:
I began to pick on Nancy Schultz, the class coward. A
timid child, afraid of everything, she'd been marked as a
sissy from the beginning of grade school. One day she and
I were two of the last stragglers left on the school playground in the late afternoon. She feared the long steel slide
more than anything, afraid of its height and the speed one
gathered traveling down it. Nevertheless, I approached her
and bullied her into climbing up its stairs and sliding
down its slick expanse, which must have seemed very long
to her. She cried, she whimpered, she begged me to leave
her alone, but I persisted until she landed in a heap at
the slide's bottom. This act also made me feel very guilty. I
couldn't understand why I'd been so cruel.

But whatever discomforts I suffered during this time—
questions about my own conduct, loneliness for Mother,
rejection by Ellen—they were eased in large measure when
I lay beside my father in bed. As he caressed me, he told me

I was sweet, lovable, his pal. And I felt secure, safe. The slight queasiness occasioned by his admonitions to secrecy and by that peculiar voice he sometimes used seemed inconsequential compared to the solace he gave me. Our time in bed, fondling and talking, seemed a natural extension of the companionship that had developed between us.

In 1953 my father turned forty and began to feel some of the attitudes connected with what is now called the mid-life crisis. Several years earlier he'd been pleased to get a state job that offered security and predictability. It suited his temperament, giving him a chance to enforce the rules and wear the uniform he prized so highly. It satisfied his limited ambition. He always claimed that his lack of a college education held him back professionally. But that was probably a convenient excuse for him to avoid the kind of competition he wouldn't have had the stomach for in any case. He'd opted for steadiness and safety in his job. Now, however, he saw this same work, which was not particularly satisfying, stretching before him for another twenty-five years, a rather gloomy prospect.

His body was also beginning to reflect the passage of time. In the summer of 1953, when he took us swimming at Green Lake, his body looked very different in swimming trunks than it had the summer before. It was thicker through the middle, his chest fleshier, the thighs of his well-shaped legs softer. His hair, too, was changing, darkening in color and growing sparser. And his eyes were taking on a strange cast, somewhat unfocused, slightly veiled.

Never articulate or outgoing, he now turned still further inward, establishing the habit of sitting for long stretches in his rocking chair, rocking monotonously, empty eyes staring straight ahead, shrouded in silence but with an air of discontent hovering about him.

My body, too, had begun to change. I was ten years old, beginning to develop breasts and hating them. The complete tomboy, I felt very uncomfortable with these new additions. They could only hinder me as I ran bases, shinnied up trees, raced with my dog through the empty fields that stretched out behind our house. I tried to cover them by wearing baggy clothes in many layers. But even that didn't prevent me from acquiring a new nickname: Chesty.

My sexual curiosity was growing also, and Mother's stabs at sex education, encompassed in two cursory and uncomfortable conversations, had raised more questions than they'd answered.

When I was eight she admonished me to break the habit of sitting on my father's lap.

"You're too big for that," she said. "It causes things to happen that shouldn't, and you cause it, so don't do it."

Nowhere in these two sentences could I find anything which made me understand why it was wrong, or anything to allay my curiosity about what it was I'd sometimes felt when Dad held me on his lap. But I did stop doing it.

Her other effort was addressed to Ellen and me together. Clearly disconcerted, her mouth tight with an exaggerated seriousness, she approached us one day and fired her question.

"Do you girls know about sex and having babies?"

"Of course, Mother," Ellen replied. "We studied it in school, and Barbara Rapp told me everything she knows."

Mother nodded, the beginnings of relief softening the set of her jaw.

"What about you, Kathy? What do you know?" she asked.

Self-conscious myself, hating to see her terrible discomfort, I quickly mimicked my sister.

(2 5)

"Everything," I said. "Ellen told me all about it."

"Do either of you have any questions?" Mother asked.

I did, but I didn't want to prolong the agony another moment. Ellen and I silently shook our heads.

"Well then, that's fine. . . ." Her voice trailed off and the subject was closed.

Eventually, during a film about menstruation that was shown in school, I learned that men had sperm and women had eggs, and when sperm and egg met, a baby resulted. I also learned that the act which caused this was called sexual intercourse.

Meanwhile, in the bed in the spare room, I continued to teach myself nameless things. Using different techniques, I discovered, caused different feelings. I learned to intensify and prolong the pleasure. Sometimes while I was touching myself, pictures of Dad popped into my head.

In the spring of 1954 my mother's father died. Mother said she wanted us all to say good-bye to our grandfather. So the day after receiving the news, the whole family traveled down-home to Mayfield and the Hinkle farm.

I had never seen a dead person, and I didn't particularly want to see one. But, of course, if Mother wanted me to, I was glad to pretend I did.

Grandpa Hinkle was lying in the front room of the house where I had spent so many summer nights. Baskets of flowers lined the walls and filled every corner, their odor heavy in the air. I stood in line with Ellen and Andrew and several of my cousins, waiting my turn to approach Grandpa's body, remembering a scene in the milkhouse several summers before. I'd come running in to find Grandpa Hinkle urinating in the drain. Hearing me approach, he quickly turned his back. I was curious about what I'd seen and moved closer. As I did he just kept turning, keeping his back to me, making it impossible for me to see what he was doing, never saying a word.

I could make no connection between that man and the stiff gray figure lying before me now. When I touched his hand, it was cold. I alternated between wanting to giggle and wanting to whimper with fear. I felt very little grief. The thing that finally did make me cry was hearing my grandmother's lament. Her sobs drifted on the springtime air into the yard where her grandchildren were playing, and I thought they were the saddest sounds I'd ever heard.

Sometime that summer Dad discovered my breasts. The air was warm, and I remember his hands sticking to my skin as they moved from my back to my chest.

"Katy," he exclaimed, his delight evident, "what have you got here?"

I hesitated, uncertain how to answer.

"Oh, you know what they are," I said finally.

"You're growing pretty early." His hands continued caressing my breasts. "Why, you're bigger than your ma already."

I hated his mentioning Mother, and I hated the terrible cackling sound that escaped from his mouth. At the same time, feelings were occurring in my body similar to those I experienced during my interludes in the spare room. I felt confused and frightened.

"I think I'll go back to my room now," I murmured.

"What's the matter?" he asked. "Does it bother you that I touched your tits?"

I'd never heard my father use a word like "tits." His language was always very proper, and he had an ironclad rule against swearing, disapproving even of certain slang expressions.

I felt his arm slide off my back as I moved slowly and silently away from the bed.

"You know, Katy, it's real hard for me not to touch you."

His voice pulled me back. I despised its sound, but I loved the words it uttered.

"You're such a good-looking, sweet little thing, so affectionate, so pleasing. You're so different from your crabby ma."

I had returned to the bedside, and his hands reached up to stroke me.

"I love you so much, Katy. You know I'd do anything for you, and I know you want to please me too. But some people don't think I should touch you like this, especially your ma. So it's best for her if you don't tell her."

"Why doesn't she think it's okay?"

"She's naive about these things, probably because her upbringing was so strict. I think it's good for girls to learn things from their fathers, but everybody doesn't think the way I do."

I wondered what "naive" meant, but I didn't ask. I wondered why people disagreed about these things, but I didn't ask that either. I just stood there, tugged between the poles of pleasure and fear, while his hands moved over my body.

Of course I wouldn't tell Mother, I decided. That would make him mad and they'd probably fight about it. We'd had enough of that. I just wanted things to be peaceful.

"The only way we can hurt anybody, Katy, is if we tell them," he said to me. "Otherwise, who are we hurting?"

I supposed that was true. Touching me seemed to please

Dad enormously, and I liked being able to do that. Mother didn't know even though I often had a desire to tell her. The sensations his hands produced in me felt good. Now when I masturbated, which was more and more often, I always pictured him in my head.

He now focused exclusively on my breasts when I crawled into bed with him several times a week. Slowly unbuttoning my pajama top, he stretched one of his large hands between my nipples, playing a game he'd devised of "wiring" them together, teasing me, knowing I was aroused. My sexual curiosity was intense, and he knew that. So was my fear.

"I'm scared, Daddy," I'd say to him.

"I'll take care of you, Katy," he always replied. "You don't have to be afraid."

"When is Mother coming back?" I'd ask.

"Don't you worry about her," he'd say. "What she don't know can't hurt her."

When occasions arose for me to be away from home, I felt relieved. They meant I'd have some distance from Dad. During the fifth grade I had my appendix removed, and my nights in the hospital were like a vacation from him. I now welcomed summer visits to relatives; they were reprieves from his relentless attention.

Still, when I was home I sought out that attention as avidly as ever. My need to please him and to receive the emotional reassurance he was willing to give me in return was so much greater than the uneasiness I felt. When his strange, cooing voice bothered me, the tenderness of his words erased my misgivings. When he touched my breasts, comparing them favorably to Mother's, my qualms were quieted by the comfort his gentleness gave me. *This* man, the one beside me in bed, was so much nicer than the exacting and austere authority who stalked about in the other rooms of the house, or the torpid figure who sat rocking for hours at a time, staring into space. Who wouldn't want to make *this* man appear as often as possible?

My father and I came to each other out of great neediness. I wanted emotional sustenance, an assurance of love, an obliteration of the fear of abandonment. He wanted sexual gratification, perhaps to ease the pain of his own emptiness, to deny the inexorable movement of time, to assuage his bruised ego. And in a sense, at that time we served each other very well.

CHAPTER

3

"I tried to teach you everything I knew about life."

—*Dad*

By the middle of the sixth grade I had begun to listen to Mother's repeated pleas that I clean my nails, comb my hair, put on fresh clothing each day. I had also begun to notice boys as something other than fellow team members and competitors in the athletic arena. On the class camping trip in the spring of 1956, I took up with my first boyfriend, Sheldon Carlson.

Our romance consisted of his riding alongside me on the two and a half miles between school and my house, smiling at me across the room in the classes we shared, going together to a few parties where we played kissing games, and writing me a single letter from the camp he went off to in June. I was glad to have Sheldon, even though I wasn't especially attached to him.

And I felt rather the same way about Josie Eichstra,

my best friend. I was glad to have a "best friend"; I knew you were supposed to, that it was normal. And I had Josie, even though I was never particularly comfortable with her. The one time I stayed overnight at her house I felt very shy and ill at ease with both her and her parents. I remember wishing I could be relaxed and smiling with them, but finding it impossible. I remember not getting up all night long to go to the bathroom because I was afraid someone would hear me. The entire experience was quite unpleasant, and I never repeated it.

Even though I'd cleaned myself up and begun to behave more like a girl, Ellen still hadn't much use for me. Or for the rest of the household. She avoided family occasions whenever possible, stayed away from the house as much as she could, and stuck to her room when she was there. She spent hours in seclusion, listening to records, painting her nails, fussing with her hair.

She couldn't escape, however, when either the Hinkle or Crosley family got together. Mother and Dad demanded she be present. And as much as she hated these gatherings, I loved them.

I was fascinated by the differences between the families. The Hinkles were workers and prayers who didn't drink, dance, curse, or spend time on frivolities. At their house we always had to be on our best behavior, and were amply rewarded for it by warm and loving praise and wonderful food at Sunday dinner. The Crosleys, on the other hand, were a cardplaying, beer-drinking, storytelling crowd who always seemed to be having fun. When they drank beer the Crosleys also ate crackers and smelly Limburger cheese. Dad, who was a very moderate drinker, always followed an exact ritual when he had a glass of beer. He poured it very slowly, knowing when to stop so that the head foamed up over the rim of the glass but never ran down the side. He let it sit until the bubbles rose to the top and the foam disappeared. Then he drank it, also slowly. I loved watching him go through the whole lengthy process.

Late in the spring of 1956 Dad committed himself to a new and better job in another part of the state. That fall he was to become a training officer at Three Forks Juvenile Reformatory in Great Rapids. Mother, who'd left her job at the hospital but devoted even longer hours to the "special cases" she'd taken on, was agreeable to the move but hadn't much time to give to preparing for it. Packing and its attendant chores—first cousins to housework—were not her cup of tea anyway.

Perhaps the impending changes in job and geography lightened Dad's spirits that summer and made him seem less dour. And it was a happy time for me, unclouded by Dad's advances, which ceased in the midst of the upheaval caused by packing and the move.

He taught Andy and me to swim that summer, an accomplishment he proudly reported to anyone who would listen. At least twice a week he packed a picnic lunch, loaded me, Andy, and sometimes a very reluctant Ellen into our old blue Plymouth, and traveled to one of several nearby lakes. I always felt safe in the water, certain of myself, with his hands held like a net beneath me while I learned to breathe properly, to propel myself. Often, looking back toward the lake's edge, I saw Ellen, solitary, alien, sunning herself near our picnic spot. She was afraid of the water and wouldn't permit Dad to hold her afloat as he did Andy and me. She wouldn't let him touch her at all.

Now fourteen, Ellen was allowed to baby-sit with Andy

and me on those rare occasions when my parents went out with each other. One such evening, shortly after my folks had left, Ellen announced that some friends of hers were coming by. Her friends, at this point, were a group of greasy, foulmouthed kids she'd met up with on the school bus, and the three who showed up that night were clearly drawn from this crowd: two spindly boys with oily hair slicked back from their pimple-dotted faces and a morose young girl who looked untidy and unwashed. Frightened by their forbidden presence, as well as their rather threatening appearance, I fled to the bedroom, leaving the door open just enough to be able to hear what went on downstairs.

"Hey, you got any booze?" one of the boys asked my sister.

"Sure," she answered. "My old man keeps a bottle. Want some?"

My heart stopped when she made the offer. Couldn't she ever just keep her mouth shut! Now she'd really get it.

"But he's not much of a boozer and he'll notice if it's gone," she continued. "He'll kill me if he thinks I drank it."

"No problem," said the other boy. "Just mark the bottle, fill it with water, and he'll never know."

Ellen obviously complied, as I heard glasses clink together and one of the boys proposed a toast "to the old man."

"Hey, where'd your little sister go?" The girl's voice this time.

"That chickenshit?" said Ellen. "Hiding in her room, afraid of you guys. Afraid we'll both get it for having you in the house."

"When'll your folks be back?" asked a boy.

"Not until late," Ellen assured him. "They went to a wedding."

"Let's go tell your sister to keep quiet about the booze," one of the boys proposed. "Okay?"

I heard them mounting the stairs, heard their footsteps in the hall. Feigning sleep, I pulled the covers up around my neck.

"Hey, Kathy baby," Ellen jeered, "I know you're not asleep. Open those big blue eyes and say hi to my friends."

I lay unmoving as her friends snickered.

"You brat," she said, her voice even harder now, "if you know what's good for you, you better not tell Mom and Dad."

I remained frozen in place, eyes squeezed shut, and after what seemed an eternity the foursome shuffled out of the room and back downstairs. Soon afterward cigarette smoke and the punch lines of dirty stories floated up to me, Ellen contributing to the latter with as much gusto as the rest of them. Then, some time later, a door slammed, I heard the shriek of squealing automobile tires, and the house grew silent.

Creeping downstairs, I reached the kitchen just as my parents entered the back door, home early from the wedding.

"How come it's smoky in here?" my father asked. "And why aren't you kids in bed? What's been going on?"

"Nothing," Ellen replied, unfazed by Dad's salvo of questions. "Nothing at all."

"Don't you lie to me, Ellen. Who's been here?"

"Nobody." She was icy calm, already an accomplished liar. "Kathy lit some matches."

"I did not," I squeaked. "It's a lie. She had her friends over and they were smoking and drinking."

The look Ellen flashed me promised revenge. Dad went to the cupboard, tasted the contents of the whiskey bottle, then turned and hit Ellen so hard she banged up against the kitchen wall, surprise flooding her face before she landed in a heap, crying.

"Thomas," Mother hollered, "you'll hurt her!"

"She oughta be hurt, the little slut."

"That's no way to talk," Mother admonished him. "She just had her friends over. What's wrong with that?"

"You have no idea what she's up to," he said. "But I do. I saw her last week at the dance, teasing the boys like a whore."

"What do you mean, you saw her?" Mother was bewildered.

"He doesn't trust me and he won't leave me alone." Ellen's sobs had diminished to a whimper. "He followed me to the dance like I was a little kid, and all my friends saw him hiding behind a post in the gym, spying on me."

"Oh, Tom, for Pete's sake," Mother sputtered.

"Okay, okay. Get on your high horse if you want, but I know what she's up to."

"He followed me to the movies, too." Ellen looked first at Mother, then at Dad.

"What?" Mother was shocked.

"I intend to keep an eye on the little slut, and I'll follow her anywhere I want to. Now I'm not going to talk about this anymore." He stalked out of the room, leaving behind the echo of his thundering voice.

Later on, after lying for some time in the silence of our room, I whispered to Ellen.

"Are you asleep?"

"No, I'm not."

At least the taunting edge was gone from her voice. The incident with Dad must have canceled out her annoyance with me.

"What are you doing?"

"Thinking how mad I am at the old man. I hate him, Kathy, I really do. He's weird . . . no, he's more than weird, he's sick. And I'm gonna get away from him. You just wait and see. I'm gonna get away, and I'm gonna do it soon."

I didn't pay much attention to Ellen's pledge. She never had anything good to say about either of our parents, so this outburst wasn't too unusual.

The house we finally settled on in Great Rapids was that staple of postwar Middle American architecture, the three-bedroom ranch. Ours, however, unlike most such houses, which are built in clusters and lined up one after another along newly created streets, was a true incongruity, sandwiched between a crumbling old farmhouse and a stucco that looked as though it belonged in a Western movie.

Nothing ever seemed quite normal with us, I lamented. We were always a little different. On a street of houses we had lived in a trailer. In a big house in the country we didn't use half the rooms. Our clothes were secondhand or handmade by Mother. I didn't want to stick out, but I always felt I did. The bright red briefcase Mother bought for me that fall was a perfect symbol. No one else would have one, and I would be conspicuous. Everyone would see me as the outsider I felt myself to be. *Poor little Kathy.*

To counteract this, I set out immediately to ingratiate myself with a clique where I felt acceptance was likely, one just beneath the elite level which I shunned as an impossibility. I joined the Cooley Junior High School band as a drummer, a year of experience in Hartland behind me, this the perfect instrument for me, as sticks cost only two dollars. I went after school to the Bee Hive with a group of girls and sat around drinking Coca-Cola and giggling about the boys. I picked on members of the clique beneath ours, finding fault with what they wore, how they talked, where they lived.

Ellen, on the other hand, following her pattern, sought out the roughest crowd Cooley could offer. She scared me now with her toughness, and I disliked her associates. They were, in fifties parlance, "hoods."

One of them, Bucky Foster, was quite smitten with Ellen. Compact and muscular, attired always in his uniform of jeans, brown leather jacket, and loafers, Bucky liked to demonstrate his devotion by making daily appearances on our street, passing the house in his 1949 Ford coupe, making a three-hundred-and-sixty-degree turn at the corner, gunning the engine, and squealing away, laying rubber for fifty feet.

Impressed, Ellen began to reciprocate, harping on Bucky's resemblance to Elvis Presley, mooning over the latter's rendition of "Heartbreak Hotel" and "You Ain't Nothin' But a Hounddog," blasted out of our single-record player at full volume.

"Doesn't he remind you of Elvis?" she'd ask me frequently, noting Bucky's curly hair and the fact that he was older, seventeen years to her fourteen.

Soon they were together constantly, riding around in his car, going to the movies, hanging out at the root beer stand afterward, spending hours sitting in our driveway, masked by the Ford's steamy windows. Their alliance provoked bitter quarrels between my parents.

"Thomas, you cannot allow her to go out with that boy," Mother contended. "She's bound to get into trouble."

"Then she deserves to," he'd reply. "I'm tired of policing her. Let her learn to take the hard knocks in life like everybody else."

Dad's alienation from Mother, and from himself, deepened rapidly once we were settled in Great Rapids. He
was more morose than ever. His day began at six-thirty,
when he crept into our rooms, rubbing us awake with his
huge hands, gurgling with a kind of baby talk. Andy,
who was eight, seemed still to enjoy this sort of attention. I,
unwilling to make waves, tried to accept it with indifference. Ellen loathed it. After fixing us breakfast, which
Ellen invariably refused, he went off to the reformatory,
where he policed other people's children (the offenders
were aged sixteen to thirty), returning home at three in
the afternoon, uninterested in doing anything once he'd
seeded the lawn and put in a small garden in the backyard. He made no new friends; he had no hobbies. He was
alone, rocking in his chair, producing a clucking sound as
he moved back and forth, until we began to wander in
one at a time in the late afternoon. Mother, proud of her
new job working with a doctor in private practice, anxious
to prove herself by putting in long hours, once again was
frequently absent. Dad usually cooked our dinner, fussing
over us like a mother hen.

His physical deterioration was accelerating as well. His
cheeks had sagged into jowls, his chin had doubled, his
belly had expanded into a paunch.

I don't know why Dad didn't approach me during this
period, or how I would have responded if he had. Perhaps
things were too unsettled for him to establish a routine.
Perhaps, as I've often fantasized, he was attempting advances toward Ellen. Whatever the reasons, the hiatus
afforded me a period of relative normality.

My best friend, Marilyn Winkler, and I took up with
two boys who were best friends, and the four of us joined
Y-Teens and attended all the YWCA functions together.

At church I had another group of friends, members of Methodist Youth Fellowship, and I spent Sundays and MYF retreat weekends with them. I never really liked the church itself, a modern cinder-block building that doubled as a Boy Scout center during the week. I always wished it were more elegant, wished it had pews instead of folding chairs, wished the congregation were not so unrelievedly lower-middle-class. But nevertheless I went faithfully, studied my Sunday school lessons diligently, prayed that I be shown God's will, and tried to keep my slightly superior feelings under wraps. I felt certain that it was not God's will for me to masturbate, and I rarely did it.

Privacy was at a premium in the new house, anyway. I shared a bedroom with Ellen, and it was next door to Mother and Dad's. Andy's bedroom and the only bathroom were across the hall, which led into the living room. A small dining ell and the kitchen adjoined that. Anything going on in one room of the house could be heard in any other.

Mother and Dad were sometimes home together in the evening, but this didn't seem to make them any closer. I remember a frequent exchange between them at this time. I think I knew even then that they were talking about sex, although it was never mentioned.

"Ma," he would say, about nine-thirty or ten o'clock, "let's go to bed."

"I'll be there soon," she'd reply. "You go on ahead."

"What're you gonna do? Stay up all night?"

"I want to finish this sweater I'm knitting" (or book I'm reading or television program I'm watching).

"That's crap! The best thing for you is rest, gal."

"Oh, Tom, get over it! I'm staying up."

In the winter of 1957–58, I was in the middle of the eighth grade, Ellen halfway through the tenth. Still inseparable from Bucky, she suddenly began accepting the hearty breakfasts Dad had been trying to force on her for years, often eating pancakes, eggs, toast, and bacon in a single sitting. At night she drank chocolate malts. My parents noticed the drastic change in her eating habits but simply chided her for overdoing, refusing to acknowledge the warning signs. The school got in touch with Mother: Ellen had used up all her sick days but was still missing classes. Mother professed to be baffled. She saw her daughter leave every day for school. Where else would she go? When Ellen began to vomit each morning, losing her big breakfast in the halls of Central High, Mother still refused to confront the issue, ascribing the disturbance to a flu bug or an allergy. Only when a doctor told her her daughter was five months pregnant did she cease dodging.

But, still unwilling to deal with the consequences of this shattering news, Mother forced Ellen to face Dad alone, arranging to be out for the evening. He was enraged and banished Ellen from the house, literally pushing her into the night and locking the doors. When Mother finally returned, she was furious.

"She needs us now more than ever," she screamed at him. "Don't you understand that?"

"She's a no-good tramp," he hollered back. "I don't want her in this house."

"We can't just let her run away. We have to help her."

"Help her, help her." He mimicked Mother mockingly. "No one can help her. Let her take care of herself."

"Tom, we're all she's got." Now Mother's tone was pleading.

"Who's she pregnant by?"

"Bucky, of course."

"Well, it's all your fault. You let him hang around."

"I did not!" She was outraged again. "It's your fault. You let them sit around outside in that car until all hours doing God knows what."

When they finally stopped flaying each other and set out to look for Ellen, they found she'd gone to Bucky's and crawled into the house through his bedroom window. A meeting between the two sets of parents was scheduled for the following day.

With Ellen and Bucky watching from the sidelines, the Fosters and Crosleys waged a battle over their children's future. Catholic and proud, the Fosters were reluctant to absorb this fifteen-year-old outsider into their family. How could they even be certain their boy was responsible? The Crosleys, not nearly as united, put forward separate cases. No child of hers was going to have an abortion, Mother said, even if it meant she had to raise the child herself. There was no way he would raise another man's child, Dad countered, saying he intended to sue Bucky for rape. The compromise agreement they ultimately came to was that Ellen and Bucky would wed immediately, Bucky to leave soon thereafter for six months' Army duty in South Carolina, Ellen to live at home while she awaited the baby's birth and Bucky's return, the latter at Mother's insistence and to Dad's great dismay.

He no longer wanted the responsibility for his daughter, a feeling that must have been related to the years of rebuffs she'd handed him. She belonged to another man; let him take care of her. He liked neither Bucky nor his parents. They weren't good enough for a child of his, however badly she'd turned out. He also didn't want a baby in the house. But still, grudgingly, he went along, knowing that if Mother was determined he really had no choice.

Dad, of course, made all of us pay for his capitulation, exhibiting his disapproval whenever possible, fueling the tension in the house so that it remained at a nearly unbearable level. Ellen had to quit school and was always at home, a constant reminder of the family shame no matter how withdrawn she became. Mother and Dad had to undergo the ordeal of informing relatives and friends of their daughter's disgrace. They barely spoke to each other. And I knew, without any prompting, that it was now incumbent upon me to be smarter, cleaner, more popular, more accomplished, to compensate for Ellen's fall. My desire to please was no longer just a preference; it was now a voracious need.

Despite these pressures, many omens were good as I began the ninth grade in the fall of 1958. I was fourteen years old, and at last I had my own room. When Ellen and her baby boy had departed in June, I'd immediately re-arranged it to suit me, piling my several stuffed animals and an oversized rag doll on her old bed, getting my records out of the closet and arranging them on shelves which had held her things, taking over her desk and filling the bulletin board above it with pictures from magazines, church programs, snapshots, and other items I deemed significant.

One day in late September, I had followed my usual school-night routine of studying from seven to nine and taking a bath, brushing my teeth, and putting on my pajamas before going to bed about nine-thirty. I liked this time of night, when it was quiet, with Andy asleep already, the television off, Mother sewing or reading, Dad reading or getting ready for bed himself. Mother was away this night, and I'd already said goodnight to Dad before going into my room.

When I crossed to the window to pull down the shade, I was caught by a scene in the farmhouse next door. Lit by an exposed bulb in the ceiling fixture, a young man and woman writhed on the bed, their naked bodies entangled. Fascinated, I stood unmoving, gazing at the spectacle outlined by our neighbor's window. I thought how strange it was that they weren't doing this later at night, in the dark, as I knew my parents did. I also thought, So that's how you do it, and I felt aroused watching them.

"You like watching that, Katy?"

Dad's voice caused me to start, and I reached up to yank down the shade.

"I was just pulling this down."

"You don't have to kid me."

I could feel he'd moved closer; I still faced the now-shuttered window.

"I know you were looking. You'd like to get a piece of that, wouldn't you?"

An embarrassed laugh spurted from my mouth. Quickly I cut it off.

"You know," he went on, "I think we should have a little talk. I'm afraid that what happened to Ellen will happen to you."

"You don't have to worry about me, Dad." I turned to face him, a tall figure dressed only in his pajama bottoms. I was still flustered but tried to sound assured. "I know enough not to get pregnant. I don't want to get married."

(44)

"That doesn't mean you can't have sex, Katy. It just means you have to be careful. You have to know how to do it and who to do it with."

What an astonishing idea to come from my father, the enforcer of rules! Before I could even begin to absorb it, he continued.

"Doesn't it get you excited when you see naked people making love, like the two over there?"

"Well ... I suppose so ... a little." This was a disconcerting revelation to make but, after hesitating, I felt I really hadn't a choice. After all, he was my father; I was compelled to tell him the truth. And yes, it was interesting to watch those people. And yes, it did excite me.

"Remember when you used to crawl into bed with me, Katy?"

Silently, I nodded.

"You enjoyed that, didn't you?"

My discomfort made speech almost impossible. "Mmmm ... I guess so."

"I miss you sleeping with me, Katy. We could still do it when your ma's not around. She'll never know."

"It scares me, Dad. It's not right, you know."

"Who says?" His voice now assumed the same oozing quality it had had when I used to crawl into bed with him. "You're my favorite girl, Katy, and I want to show you what this sex stuff is all about. I don't want you to get hurt. I don't want you to let those boyfriends of yours get to you."

"I won't, Dad." I sounded firm, even though the night before Larry Laughlin had nearly managed to slide his hand inside my bra while we sat in the front seat of his car. Sweet, gentle, my first date who had his own car; I'd been afraid to stop him. The couple in the back seat were doing whatever they wanted. I hated to make a fuss.

"Did you ever see one as big as mine?"

I was dragged back into the present by the sound of my father's voice and the sight of his penis jutting out from the fly of his pajama pants. He pulled me close to him, his hands on my shoulders. He pressed himself tight against me. His whistling breath was the only sound in the room.

I stood absolutely still, letting him hold me, not knowing what else to do. The sensation of his body next to mine felt good. It also felt wrong.

He led me to the bed and gently pushed down on my shoulders until I was sitting. He unbuttoned my pajama top and placed his fingers on my nipples, twisting, turning. He ran his hands over my breasts, down my body, underneath my pajama bottoms. He kissed my face, neck, breasts. This also felt good—and even more wrong and alarming. Pleasure and guilt, from the very beginning.

"Dad, don't!" I jumped up and moved away from the bed. "Please leave me alone."

"Aw, Katy, it's all right. I know you like it. I always knew you were a little hot-pants. Come on back here . . . I won't hurt you. I promise I won't hurt you."

His voice was seductive. He was my father and I loved him. This was his way, I supposed, of showing he loved me. He didn't want me to go through what Ellen had endured. Neither did I want to. If he showed me all about sex, then I'd know. Just one time and that'll be that, I thought. Then I'll know.

"Let me show you just this once." He echoed my thought, his voice cajoling. "We won't go all the way. Let me just tell you what to do."

"Won't Mother be home soon?"

"She called to say she'll be late. Katy, let me show you just this once."

I moved back toward the bed, reluctance bowing to curiosity and my desire to please. He undid my pajama bottoms and pulled them down around my knees. Then he wrapped my hands around him, telling me to watch while his penis grew, crooning tales of how it worked when he was with Mother, where it went, how it felt. His hands began touching my body again. He fastened his mouth for a moment on my breast, then brought it up to my mouth, kissing me. I was repelled by his wet lips, the feel of his crooked front teeth between them. I twisted my head to the side.

His hands moved to my vagina, found my clitoris, rubbed over it back and forth. I wanted to run and I wanted to stay. He told me to touch him again while his fingers continued brushing me. I did. His mouth returned to my breasts, each sucking motion sending exquisite feelings through me, pinning me in place, obliterating the desire to run, bringing me, finally, to climax.

The instant that happened, guilt and shame flooded in, pushing away the pleasure.

"Don't let go of me yet," he urged, continuing to pump himself up and down in my hand until a thick liquid spilled out and ran down the leg of his pajamas. Then he lay still, a smile spread across his face.

When I moved to get up, he drew me back with an affectionate hug and softly kissed my cheek.

"Thanks, Katy," he murmured. "Thanks so much."

CHAPTER

4

"I couldn't conceive that a man who locked up thieves and murderers could have done what he did. I kept thinking how dirty he made me feel about having to get married."

—*Ellen*

Later that night, awake in bed, savoring my relief that Dad's sex lesson was over, I heard Mother come in.

"Hi, Lou," Dad greeted her, his voice soft and pleasant, much nicer than usual. "Glad you're home. It must have been important for Dr. Hodgman to keep you so late."

He rarely showed interest in her work or gave her an opportunity to talk about it, and she seized it gratefully. I heard her droning on for some time while Dad made patient listening noises.

The next morning I lingered in my room, reluctant to see Mother, afraid she'd know what had happened just by looking at me. My heart pounded and my stomach felt fluttery as I approached the kitchen, where she was gulping down a cup of coffee before leaving for work.

"Hi, Mom," I said, trying to sound ordinary, hoping my voice wouldn't shake.

"Kathy, would you stop at the dry cleaner's after school and pick up this coat for me?" She handed me a pink slip, took a final swallow of coffee, and headed out the door, her air of distraction as impenetrable as ever. Clearly, she knew nothing.

That day in school I watched to see if friends looked at me differently. Perhaps they would discern some invisible mark, some obscure sign. But they treated me as they always had.

By the end of the day my anxiety was greatly diminished. No one knew. That was obvious. It had been awful, a terrible thing to do, but at least it was past. It would never happen again. Dad seemed happier. What a change—and a relief—from the withdrawn, unresponsive personality he'd exhibited for so long. And who knew, maybe I *had* learned something. Anyway, the point was, it was over and no harm done.

I was happy that week. I loved the feeling of deepening autumn, the smell of burning leaves wrapping round me in the soft afternoon air as I walked home from school, each day a little more chill in the oncoming darkness. When Mother was late another night that week, Dad didn't seem annoyed. And one night, when she actually got home a little early and we all had dinner together, he asked again about her work and listened to her reply. Both Mother and Dad were more relaxed than usual, the way I'd always wished they would be. We seemed like a normal family, sitting together at the dinner table, talking to each other.

On Saturday morning I was straightening up my room when I heard Mother leave on her usual round of errands. Then I heard Dad giving Andy some change, suggesting he pick up his friend Billy on the way to the candy store and take him to play in the park at the end of the street. Then I heard Dad calling me.

"K-K-K-Katy." His voice came down the hall. "Where are you, girl?"

"In my room," I answered, wondering what he wanted.

He appeared in the door, a funny grin on his face, his eyes somewhat cloudy, an obvious bulge at the front of his pants.

"Let me show you something, Katy." He spoke in that telltale voice, and I understood at once what was on his mind.

"No, Dad," I said quickly, afraid to rebuff him but more afraid of doing again what we'd done several nights before.

"If I show you these things, Katy, you won't get in trouble like your sister did."

"I'm not going to get in trouble, Dad."

"Let me show you, girl. It's better for you to learn from me."

"Please Dad," I pleaded with him. "It's not right."

"Who says?" he scoffed. "What's so wrong about it?"

I was beginning to feel a little desperate. "I know right from wrong," I said, as firmly as I could, "and this is wrong. What would Mother think?"

"She's never gonna find out." He smiled at me now. "If nobody knows, who are we hurting?"

I couldn't answer him. I stood mute. In the silence he crossed the room, touched me, showed me again how to touch him, and directed us through the same sexual scene we'd played before. My feelings were the same: I was aroused and I was ashamed. The result was the same: he was pleased and he was pleasant for several days afterward.

Our sexual contact quickly fell into a distinct routine,

something I refused to face for quite some time, preferring instead to believe that each time was the last. Dad always made sure the house was empty and locked. This was most easily accomplished on Saturday mornings, when Mother was out and Andy could be easily persuaded to go out and play. Even so, it was never entirely safe. Sometimes Mother forgot something and returned. Sometimes Ellen came by and I'd have to run to the door in my robe. I wondered if they ever noticed that Dad was always in the bathroom. When they asked about the locked door, I made up an elaborate story about my newly developed fear of being in an unlocked house. To cover me, Dad made a house rule that doors must be kept locked at all times.

He always bathed first, running the water slowly into the tub, lathering his body, carefully rinsing it off, emerging finally like a bridegroom from a ritual bath. Then came the verbal approach, made in that low cooing voice I detested, his eyes glazed over with a film of desire.

At first he emphasized his wish to help me.

"I can teach you everything, Katy," he'd say. "Then you'll never be in the position Ellen was."

Gradually, as time passed, he began more and more to stress his own need.

"You gotta take care of me, Katy," he'd say. "I just need more than your ma can give me. I don't know what will happen if I don't have you."

Sometimes he'd tell me stories of women he'd had, mostly apocryphal, I believe, or sexual scenes he'd witnessed in the Army. But whatever his tactics, they were effective. I'd become excited, hooked.

Seeing my interest, he'd hurry to the bathroom and return with a towel, which he spread beneath him on the bed. Aware that he could easily arouse me by fondling or sucking my breasts, he'd focus on them first. Then, already erect from his own excitement, he'd rub his penis over my clitoris, slowly, up and down. Finally, he would enter me with his fingers and guide me to a climax. After I was done, I'd bring him to orgasm. When that was over, grinning with satisfaction, he'd pick up the towel and take it into the bathroom, plunge it into hot water, wring it out, and hang it up to dry. I hated the sight of it, this terrible reminder in full view. I felt the odor of sperm still clung to it, filling the small room, and I was sure Mother would notice. She never did. Even more obvious, I thought, was when he used his underwear instead of a towel and threw the dirty Jockey shorts directly into the laundry. She apparently was oblivious to this also.

Dad often suggested variations on this basic sexual theme. He showed me two forms of oral sex, cunnilingus and fellatio, but I refused to repeat either, the former because I found it repugnant, the latter because it seemed to give him too much pleasure. When he encouraged me to have intercourse, describing how Mother liked to sit astride him and pump slowly up and down, I refused that also. I feared the pain from his large penis and I believed that if I didn't do *that*, perhaps my other sins—masturbation, childhood stealing, swearing, thinking bad thoughts—would be forgiven.

When I said no to something Dad always backed down quickly, letting me decide, assuring me "we'll only do what you like." He could have forced me anytime to do anything he wished. That he never did increased my confusion. His consideration of my wishes made his behavior seem loving. And at first I was insulated from the full force of my guilt and disgust by two things: my sexual curiosity and my overwhelming need for love, attention, approval. For his part, so long as I "chose" our acts, he made himself believe he was accommodating me. He prided himself on his great restraint.

From the beginning I felt the impulse to tell Mother, but always it was overruled by that passive, needy part of me which couldn't risk losing her approval. I *knew* she would believe it was my fault. She'd told me I caused things when I sat on Dad's lap. She had abandoned me before— when Andy was born, when she sent me away in the summer, when she returned to work—and I didn't want to test whether she would do it again. I knew only that I must try to please both my parents in whatever ways they prescribed. By so doing, I'd make up for Ellen, keep peace in the house, satisfy my insatiable need for endorsement.

During part of the winter I turned fifteen, I seemed to be accomplishing all these things without paying a terrible price. I continued to do well in school, as I always had. I went on dates with Larry Laughlin, but Dad didn't take him seriously enough to be jealous and I was never aroused by the adolescent level of our sexual contact. The atmosphere at home was more relaxed than it had ever been.

Gradually, however, I began to feel the relentless nature of Dad's sexual attention. His demands were becoming regular and insistent. It was harder and harder to maintain the illusion that each time would be the last. I was no longer curious. I knew now how things were done, what they felt like. I wanted him to leave me alone. Still, every time he approached me I would ultimately respond.

In the spring of that year he took me squirrel hunting

down-home. Wandering through the fields and woods of
Grandma Hinkle's farm, I remembered all the summers I'd
spent walking over this land, peaceful days except for the
ache of missing Mother, uncomplicated days of just passing
time between getting up in the morning and going to bed
at night.

"You sure are a good-looking little gal." Dad's voice,
coming from behind, broke into my reverie. "It's been an
awful long time since we done anything."

My heart began to pound, and I walked a little faster,
my feelings a confused mixture of hate, anger, love, lust.

"What's the matter?" he asked, coming up alongside me.
"Don't you like it anymore? You getting too big for your
britches?"

I glanced over at him, seeing the bulge in the front of his
brown hunting pants, knowing this meant he would insist.
I began to shake. He was my father, the father I loved so
much, needed so much. He used to make me feel safe when
I crawled into bed with him. But now this "game" we
played seemed a terrible task and it frightened me.

"You know how I need it," he said, "and you know you
like it. Let's look for a place to hide out here."

I smiled vaguely at him and walked on.

"Squirrels mate like rabbits," he said, kicking at a dead
tree stump, poking at a pile of leaves, trying to roust out any
hiding animals. "Look! There's a partridge. They mate
by squatting and shaking and fluttering their feathers. If
you keep an eye out you'll see what I mean. It's interesting
to watch.

"Here's a perfect place," he said finally, pointing with
his gun to a gentle hollow in the ground surrounded by
tall, leafy trees.

"I don't feel like it, Dad," I said softly. "Uncle Walt might see us."

"Aw, Katy, c'mon. Look at me. You can't leave me like this."

He began arranging the dry leaves in the hollow into a nest. The hot sun overhead filtered through the leaves, and it was absolutely silent.

"Walt's in the barn by now and he won't be watching for us. No one knows we're here."

He propped his gun against a tree and settled into the nest, pulling me down beside him. Reaching a hand beneath my baggy blue jeans, he was overjoyed to discover I was wet.

"Why, you little tease," he exclaimed, "you're as horny as me, aren't you? You want some, don't you?"

He didn't need to hear my muffled, sheepish affirmative to continue. He didn't need to hold me down with one of his long legs pinning mine. The thought of escaping him had never occurred to me.

I could endure this one more time, the litany began in my head. And since I had to, I might as well enjoy it. But the enjoyment was not unmixed. He sucked my breasts, and I felt wildly excited and terribly angry. He entered me with his fingers, and a surge of hate combined with desire. I tried as much as I could to hide my pleasure from him. I tried to mute my response. Still, he saw my excitement and a grin spread across his face.

"I knew you wanted it," he said. "You can't fool me."

Two weeks later Dad suggested we go hunting again. I refused.

"What's the matter, Katy?" he asked. "We had fun the last time, didn't we?"

"Yes, Dad," I answered, always the obedient daughter.

"Then what is it? You getting too grown-up?"

"No, Dad," I replied. "I just don't feel like it."

A week later he asked me again. Again I refused. As a punishment for my insolence, he took my gun away and traded it in on a .22 for Andy.

That spring he also began to respond to my increasing interest in boys. When I ruled out hunting trips for the two of us, he developed a sudden passion for family camping. In the middle of each week, as though it had just occurred to him, he'd say: "Let's all go camping this weekend. Wouldn't that be fun?"

Mother was agreeable, because it meant she'd be away from the house and the chores it represented. Andy, of course, thought it would be fun. And I was glad we were all doing something together, like a normal family. Also, although Dad often tried to corner me for quick sex during these outings, it was difficult. We were all together almost all the time.

It wasn't until we'd been on several weekend trips that I realized the main purpose of this camping program Dad had instituted was to keep me from dating—to keep me away from the boys.

One Friday night in May we'd gone to camp at a spot called The Oaks, about two hours away from home. I'd made a date for that Sunday night with Freddie Vogel. Dad complained about it all weekend.

"I don't know why you'd do such a dumb thing," he said Friday night after we'd settled in at our campsite. "Now we'll have to be back early."

"We'd be back anyway, Tom," Mother pointed out.

"Well, I don't know about that," he huffed. "I'm not so sure."

"Seems like she could have had more sense," he said Saturday, still going on about it.

"What difference does it make?" Mother asked, exasperated by his persistence.

"I just hate being tied down," he muttered.

"Well, you're not tied down very tight," said Mother. "We're always home by six anyway."

"Who knows what we might want to do?" he whined.

"Oh, for heaven's sake, Tom. I don't know what you're so concerned about. Get over it!"

"I guess we can get you back in time," he said to me Sunday morning.

"Thanks, Dad," I said, aware that an unspoken message had just passed between us.

I knew he was saying: Okay, I'll get you home for that date, but you'll have to pay me back. And I knew I was agreeing to the trade.

This was the beginning of our barter system. We began to negotiate with each other, and sex was the currency of our transactions. I was beginning to accept that I was trapped in this sexual liaison with my father, and beginning to learn to use it to my advantage.

That summer, at my urging, Dad bought a new car. A pink-and-white Pontiac Safari station wagon with whitewalls and a radio, it was hardly the sort of automobile he'd have chosen. But I loved it, and he liked pleasing me.

That summer we also bought a new house. Mother didn't want it; she thought the idea was foolhardy.

"Don't be ridiculous, Tom." She dismissed the idea when he first raised it. "We have plenty of room here. Besides, we can't afford anything larger."

But I wanted to move. I hated our house with its small rooms, tiny front yard, run-down neighborhood. Looking forward to attending Central High in the fall, I didn't want to be one of the kids from the wrong side of the tracks. I wanted as few strikes against me as possible at the beginning of my high-school career. Dad wanted to please me, so we got the new house, despite Mother's objections and the fact that it was somewhat beyond their means.

When we moved to the new house, another ranch but a roomier one on a nicer street with a large corner yard, I also insisted that we move to a new church, deciding on First Methodist, which counted among its parishioners the upper echelon of Great Rapids society.

The building itself was one of the oldest in the state, reeking of tradition, graced by two elegant spires and beautiful stained-glass windows on three sides. I loved the richness of its interior and the look of the people who attended services there. I even convinced Dad to attend, and felt especially respectable when I had a parent seated on either side of me in the pew on Sunday morning.

Appearances were becoming crucial to me. Each day that my incestuous relationship with my father continued, my commitment to the appearance of normality grew deeper. Each increase in my guilt, shame, and disgust caused an equal increase in my need to create a glossy, pleasing surface. The darker the inside, the brighter the outside must be to hide it.

I had by now an obsession with cleanliness, bathing two or three times a day, never wearing clothes more than once without washing or dry-cleaning them, shampooing my hair daily. If I looked clean, my dirty little secret wouldn't show.

I'd come to believe that I must, single-handedly, make us seem a normal, happy family. The proper house and the proper car were part of it. Keeping down the tension level in the house was another part. The way to regulate that, I knew, was sex. Sexually satisfied, Dad was agreeable, affectionate, likable. Unsatisfied, he was nasty, sullen, unreachable. I think Mother may have understood this on some level. She certainly encouraged our close relationship.

If I had a favor to ask, she sent me to him.

"You'll have to ask your father," she'd say. "It's up to him."

She urged me to spend time with him.

"Come right home after school, Kathy," she'd say. "You know how he hates to be alone."

And when they fought, she asked me to act as intermediary.

"Talk to your father, Kathy," she'd say. "You know he won't listen to me."

I maintained a pleasant facade with Mother. I wouldn't have risked losing her approval by doing otherwise. But beneath that facade, anger was simmering. I felt she should protect me from my father, not push me at him. I felt she should be able to see what was going on and put a stop to it. But she neither saw nor intervened. And the rage continued to grow.

By the time I reached high school, I had two absolutely separate personalities. The public one, exhibited to family and friends alike, was friendly, stable, honest, thoughtful, courteous, trustworthy, reliable, and cooperative. The private one was fearful, isolated, anxious, and depressed.

CHAPTER

5

"You were in my eyes someone that fit in and was successful at an early age—grades, looks, jobs, a boyfriend."

—Andy

I met Roger Brady on my first day of high school in the fall of 1959 and almost immediately felt the teenage version of falling in love. Short and stocky, his body hardened by sports, Roger had a rich brown crew cut and a flashing white smile. He also had a car, a boat, a summer cottage, and limitless spending money doled out by his well-to-do family. Despite his being a year ahead of me, we shared a math class, and it quickly became apparent that he was also interested in me.

I couldn't believe my good fortune. The Bradys owned half of Great Rapids. There couldn't be anything more *normal*, more impressive, than a relationship with Roger.

But I was worried about my father. For several months he'd been behaving like a man who had fallen in love. He was clearly enchanted with me, doting on me, doing me special favors. He solicited my opinions on everything: what necktie he should wear, where we should go to eat, what I thought of the Sunday sermon. He told me I was special, so much more communicative than Mother, so sweet and pleasing. And I played my part: buying him clothes, trying to wean him away from the handmade look into nattier outfits; cooking his favorite foods; keeping his car spotless, inside and out.

The other side of this coin was that he behaved with all the jealousy and possessiveness of a lover. Before I left to go out on a date, he stormed about the house, muttering his suspicions, threatening terrible punishment if I got into trouble. Or he sulked silently, filling the house with a kind of gloomy tension that wasn't much more pleasant than his rages. He didn't like me spending much time with my girlfriends, either, refusing to allow them to stay overnight at my house or me to go to theirs.

He objected to Roger from the beginning. Face-to-face he treated him with cool correctness. But when Roger wasn't around, Dad dismissed him as less than a "real man" because of his height. He wasn't good enough for me, Dad said. Sure, his money could buy all sorts of things, but he was just a good-for-nothing playboy.

I felt how precarious my situation was. I knew Dad could forbid me to see Roger. To preclude that possibility, I negotiated with him the most perverse of all our compacts.

Lying in my bed on a Saturday morning, I heard the house emptying.

"You be sure to fill that car with gas, Lou," Dad hollered to Mother in the driveway. Then he closed the back door.

"Andy, c'mere, boy." He summoned my brother to the kitchen. There was a low murmur of voices. Then the back door closed again and I heard Andy calling to our dog, Lady, to follow him down the street.

Next I heard the sound of running water, then splashing noises, then gurgling water disappearing down the drain. Soon after that Dad appeared in my bedroom doorway, a towel wrapped around his waist.

"I want to talk to you, Dad," I said before he could begin his buildup.

"Sure, Katy," he responded warmly, coming over to the bed. "You know you can discuss anything with me. What's on your mind?"

"I wish you liked Roger better," I said. "I don't see what you've got against him."

"Aw, he's nothing but a spoiled rich brat. You can do better than him."

"But I like him, Dad. He's really nice if you'd just give him a chance."

"Well, I don't trust him," he grumbled. "His father's a sneak and probably he is too."

"Well," I said firmly, "I like him and I like going out with him."

"I don't like you spending too much time with him, Katy. I don't want you getting in trouble."

"Oh, I won't, Dad. And I just want to see him a few times a week."

"Well, that depends on you . . . on how good you behave."

"I'll be fine, Dad," I said, reaching my hand beneath his towel. "You'll see."

We understood each other perfectly. The bargain was sealed.

And later that fall I pinned down what I felt was the other necessity for a successful high-school career: a car.

Dad took me out for a driving lesson one autumn afternoon, suggesting we stop at the Golden Horseshoe Inn for him to have a beer.

"Hey, Red." As we entered he greeted the woman behind the bar, a buxom redhead with a scarlet mouth that spread across her face in a welcoming grin.

"Hiya, Cros. How are ya?" Her voice had a rasp that came from years of cigarettes. "Who ya got here?"

"This is my girl Katherine," he said. "I call her Katy."

"Dad, please," I stammered, embarrassed he'd revealed he had a nickname for me. That seemed so childish.

"She wants me to buy her a car, Red, and I heard you want to sell that old Chevy of yours."

I was thrilled. And even more excited when Dad led me to the window and showed me the black-and-yellow convertible parked outside.

"Oh, please, can we get it?" I begged him, my head already filled with visions of me chauffeuring my girlfriends around, picking them up at their houses, pulling up in front of school, impressing everybody.

"Would you take care of it?" he asked.

"Of course I would. You know I'm real careful."

"Well"—he seemed hesitant now—"you won't be sixteen till December. Maybe it's a little early to be thinking about a car."

"But if we don't buy it now, she'll sell it," I fretted. "Somebody else will get it."

"Are you sure you know what I mean about taking care of it, Katy?" He looked at me intently over the rim of his glass. "It'll be mine and you'll have to keep it in good shape for me."

"Oh, I will, Dad. I promise." My pledge was fervent, and I was squirming around in the booth with enthusiasm. "But can I drive it to school when I turn sixteen?"

"Well," he said slowly, "that all depends."

"What do you mean?" I asked.

"If you behave like I think you should, Katy, then maybe you can drive it to school sometimes. We'll see . . . we'll play it by ear."

"You mean we're going to get it?"

"What do you think?"

I leaned the upper part of my body in his direction, then slid over toward him on the seat until my leg rested against his.

"I think we should," I said softly.

"Okay," he agreed, "it's done."

So I had the boy and I had the car. And I felt triumphant about these acquisitions. But the noninterference pact, the deals I'd arranged with my father, made me feel terribly guilty, sick. Not only was I doing this shameful thing, I was profiting from it. I knew I could get anything I wanted, so long as I was willing to pay Dad's price. And it seemed I was willing. Perhaps he was right when he implied I was responsible for the whole thing, a theme he harped on consistently.

"You're such a tease, you little hot-pants," he'd tell me. "I know you want it. You just don't want to admit it."

If I was capable of manipulating circumstances so they'd pay off for me, maybe it was all my fault. Or at the very least, how could I blame Dad for everything if I got what I wanted from it? My status as victim was called into question.

To ameliorate this guilt I determined to train myself

never to receive sexual satisfaction from him. Maybe I was using the situation for my own ends, but I didn't have to enjoy any part of it.

Toward this end, I resumed masturbating, which I'd abandoned for the most part a couple of years before as a wrong and shameful act. If I satisfied myself, I reasoned, I'd be less likely to respond to him. For a time this worked fairly well. Sometimes, however, while masturbating, I fantasized intercourse with Dad and became even more disgusted with myself.

When he and I were having sex, I tried to deny myself orgasms, doing everything possible to divorce myself from the sexual moment. I found ways to make myself absent—recalling a conversation with a neighbor, a homework assignment, a grocery list, anything antisexual—ways to go out of focus, to pretend it wasn't happening. And I also learned to pretend that it was, faking orgasms to bring episodes to an end. There were still times, however, when I succumbed to his stimulation and responded genuinely. Those were occasions for severe self-flagellation.

"How could you let it happen?" I'd berate myself. "You're sick and you're bad and you've no one to blame but yourself. You know you enjoyed it. It's obviously your fault."

The schism between my inner and outer lives was growing. At school I was the perky blonde with good grades and a big smile. I was the only girl drummer in the band, a distinction of sorts, and a favorite of the band teacher, who called me Sunshine. I made a point of trying to be the best in all my classes, and often succeeded. I especially liked Spanish and English literature. I was elected a squad leader in my gym class. I prided myself on being able to get along with everyone and on being a member of the most elite clique. I had a boyfriend who was considered a prize catch and a clutch of girlfriends who were happy to ride around in my car with me. I was a winner.

At the same time, I was growing more isolated emotionally. The contrast between this life of glossy popularity at school and my lonely, fearful life at home was becoming acute. Outside the house I was the successful, happy teenager—absorbed by my appearance, my boyfriend, school activities, gossip, grades. Inside it, I was Dad's prisoner.

When I came home in the late afternoon, he'd be waiting for me, sitting in his chair, rocking, his stomach hanging over his belt, eyes staring blankly ahead. He could be sullen or demanding or accusatory or playful. Whatever his mood, I was completely controlled by it.

To protect my public persona, to keep my life with Dad from tainting it in any way, I developed a way of relating to my friends that looked warm and friendly but seldom strayed from the most superficial level. I knew instinctively that intimacy was dangerous for me. A close relationship could lead to the revelation of my secret. I became very good at going through the motions; I shared very little of myself.

Sundays during high school were the times when I felt most vividly the contrast between my two selves. In the morning I'd sit with my family in church—Mother, Dad, me, and Andy lined up in a pew—radiating pious attention, letting the glorious music wash over me. After the service I'd greet the people in the congregation, smiling, talking, feeling their approval of my pleasing personality, my impeccable appearance. At home, during Sunday lunch, I continued to smile, chattering, discussing the sermon, recalling the hymns, recounting conversations. But when lunch was over I'd retreat to my room.

There, alone, the smile came off and fear and sadness and anger set in. I didn't know what caused these feelings, but they beset me nearly every Sunday afternoon. It was as though Sunday mornings were lit by a glorious and glowing sun; in the afternoon it was covered over by a dark, enveloping cloud. Frequently, I got through these periods of intense gloom by sitting mesmerized before the television set, sobbing over a World War II romance with Jimmy Stewart or Walter Pidgeon.

Mother began to take quite an interest in my high-school career. She immediately liked Roger and encouraged my relationship with him. She gave me extra money to buy new clothes, no longer insisting on making everything for me herself. She seemed to enjoy chatting with me about the superficial things that consumed so much of my life. And I tried desperately to establish with her what I thought was a *normal* mother-daughter relationship. I pretended that we were close.

"It's so wonderful, Mother," I'd say to her. "You and I can talk about everything."

In fact, I was as superficial with her as I was with my friends, gliding along on the surface, never touching on the unwieldy emotions that lay beneath it. What I really felt toward her was anger and a sense of betrayal. I needed her to see what was going on, but she refused. She was exercising to the fullest her gift for looking the other way. Unconsciously, she had chosen not to rock the boat, jettisoning me in the process. She was not going to jeopardize the status quo, however unsatisfactory it was, by inquiring too closely. She was not going to protect me from him.

(67)

There were times when I refused my father, and when I did, he made life nearly unbearable for all of us. Churlish, venomous, he'd spit the few words he uttered at Mother, Andy, and me, spreading a cloud of nastiness throughout the house, creating a tension that was almost palpable. I always hoped that Mother would be forced by his dreadful behavior to ask him what was wrong, rather than just attempting to tease him out of it or encouraging me to do so. I urged her to try to talk to him. Sooner or later, I felt, she'd have to ask what was behind his moods, and I wanted her to. I wanted the whole thing to blow up, blow wide open. I wanted to get rid of my terrible secret.

Once, sick to death of his meanness, his sullen silences, she did give him an ultimatum.

"You just straighten up, Tom," I heard her tell him one night in full voice, "or I'm leaving and taking the kids with me. You're making life miserable around here, and I'm plenty tired of it."

When Dad made a brief effort to behave more pleasantly, she inquired no further. This said two things to me: that she didn't really want to know what was troubling him—she demanded that he change his behavior but didn't ask what was causing it—and that she had power but wouldn't, or couldn't, use it in my behalf. I resented her terribly for both these things. I could sometimes make excuses for Dad: initial good motives, an abnormal sex drive, loving feelings for me, estrangement from Mother. But for Mother there were none. She had abandoned me again.

It was on myself, of course, that I rendered my harshest judgment. I abhorred the pleasure I took in knowing I could manipulate Dad if I chose to. I detested the weakness and passivity that kept me submitting to him. I was angry that I'd created the situation in the first place. And I must have done so. Dad said I had. He said I was curious, and I was. He said I liked the sex, and it was true—sometimes I had. And in addition to all that, if it weren't my fault surely I'd be able to tell Mother.

When I finished the tenth grade in June of 1960 I was determined to get a summer job. I didn't want to be at home all the time, available to Dad whenever he wanted me. I wanted to put more distance between us. Before approaching him, I tried to enlist Mother's support.

"There's an awful lot to do around the house, Kathy," she responded when I broached the subject.

"I know, Mother, but if I work part time I could still take care of the house too. I could do both."

"Well, you know how your father hates rattling around here by himself."

"Andy'll be here, and anyway, it's just part time."

"I don't know, Kathy. See what your father says."

"I don't want you out working, Katy," he said when I asked him. "You're too young for that. And where would you get a job anyway?"

"The supermarket needs checkout girls, and sixteen isn't too young, Dad. I'm sure you were working when you were sixteen. If I had a job I could pay room and board and have some spending money."

"You don't have to pay room and board till you're out of school," he said gently, "and I'll give you all the spending money you want."

"But I'd like to buy my own clothes and save up for college."

"Well, I don't like the idea." His voice was gruffer now.

"You're still a little girl and I want you here. You're good company for me."

"I'm not a little girl anymore, Dad," I insisted. "Please sign my application form."

Coming close to me, reaching out to touch my body, he asked, "How much will you have to work?"

"Just three afternoons a week, half days on Saturday."

"I don't like you away so much." He ran his hands over my breasts. Sensing my reticence, he added, "You don't like me touching you anymore, do you?"

I murmured something noncommittal.

"Tell you what." He continued caressing me, grinning now, showing his crooked teeth. "You be nicer to me and I'll sign your application."

"Okay," I acquiesced, fully aware of what "nicer" meant.

"But you remember," he warned, "I don't like the idea, and if you don't keep up your end of things I'll make you quit the job."

CHAPTER

6

*"Perhaps looking back on life is not the best
philosophy but we did have a lot of good times
the past ten years. I'm sure you'll agree the first
twenty weren't so bad either."*

—*Dad*

By the end of my tenth-grade year Roger and I were going
steady, his ring hanging round my neck on a chain. He was
the perfect choice for me, conservative, reserved, polite, a
"nice" boy known for his sexual restraint. I was particularly impressed by his table manners, by the relaxed way
he handled himself in a restaurant. Realizing how few
graces I possessed, I read Amy Vanderbilt's *Everyday
Etiquette,* hoping to learn what was right and proper, to
polish myself for him.

I believed I loved Roger, and often told him so. He
excited me physically when we kissed and hugged, our
only sexual contact at this time. Almost from the beginning, I'd fantasized marriage with him, knowing perhaps
that this would be the only way I'd ever escape Dad. At
the same time, as our romance progressed, it became more

and more difficult for me to relate to him at any deep level. Sometimes he could tell there was something on my mind, something I wouldn't say.

"What are you thinking, Kitty?" he'd ask, using his private name for me. "You're way off somewhere."

I thought of telling him the truth about Dad and me, but each time decided I couldn't. It was too threatening. He'd think I was deplorable, horribly sick. I could lose him by honesty, a risk I wasn't willing to take. He never forced the issue, and I was grateful for that.

It didn't bother me that Dad didn't like Roger, so long as he let me go on seeing him. And I didn't care that Roger hadn't much use for Dad. If they'd been friendly with each other it might have jeopardized my secret. Intimacy with anyone, on Dad's part or mine, could be dangerous.

And I believed this more than ever, although the idea hardly needed reinforcing, after one of the rare occasions when I participated in a slumber party given by one of my girlfriends. A group of us stayed overnight at Jane Dayton's, and I was uneasy from the beginning. This sort of occasion seemed to demand a kind of closeness that wasn't necessary during school activities or at the after-school hangout or on dates, when we each had a boy to focus on. I felt out of place; I didn't know how to conduct myself.

My uneasiness became fear when we began to play a game called Secret. Sitting in a circle, each person picked another and told something mysterious, hidden, about her. I was horrified, expecting to hear one of the girls blurt out my secret even though I knew that was impossible. What did happen was bad enough. They told me how secretive I was, how I held back. They said I was too proud, unable to accept hand-me-down clothes or a free Coke. They questioned why I never talked about my family. All of this embarrassed me greatly, and I never participated in a slumber party again.

Ellen frequently warned me to keep my distance from Roger, not to get too involved.

"The first thing you know, Kathy, you'll be married and your life will be spoiled and you'll be sorry."

At the same time, she added that she was sure I wouldn't listen to her. She didn't think her opinion carried much weight in the family, and I guess she was right. When she dropped in at the house with her baby, a common occurrence, Dad treated her like a stranger. Mother was warmer, more friendly, but she basically backed up Dad in his policy of refusing Ellen and Bucky help of any sort.

I, on the other hand, loved playing Lady Bountiful and let Ellen borrow things from me, wear my clothes, drive my car. Then sometimes, capriciously, I'd withhold these privileges, probably when I'd been asked in school if it was my sister who "had to get married," or when I'd heard her whispered about in the bathroom or the halls. When, in other words, I'd been reminded that I had to overcome her legacy of disgrace.

Andy, the pliant, undemanding child who seemed always to be in a world of his own, was now eleven years old and I was more surrogate mother than sister to him. I liked caring for him, helping him to pack his lunch, clean his room, do his minimal house chores. He was easily irritated by Dad's fussing over him. At those times he sputtered at Dad just as Mother did. I, of course, was always there to smooth everything over and keep the peace.

The sexual situation with Dad was becoming more and

more oppressive. It had gotten worse rather than better during the summer of 1960. He'd arranged a long camping trip to the Upper Peninsula of Michigan in August. During the two weeks we were there he kept up a steady stream of sexual innuendo, muttering softly to me about what he'd like to do if we were alone. On trips into town for supplies, when he insisted I accompany him, he acted out all these suggestions, pulling off the road into secluded spots where we wouldn't be seen, and sometimes touching me and urging me to touch him while we drove.

At home, when I was lying in bed and I heard him approaching, I now felt a dread that almost made me physically sick. I tried harder than ever to put myself out of reach. Sometimes I faked my period, once even presenting him with a ketchup-soaked sanitary napkin when he demanded proof. In the fall of 1960, when I began the eleventh grade, I stopped riding the bus which would deliver me home immediately after school and joined still more extracurricular activities to fill the afternoon hours. This enraged Dad. He contended I was overdoing it, that my grades would suffer, an argument he had to abandon when I continued to get all A's.

When Andy was in the house I tried to bribe him to stay put. I offered to play the games of his choice, to bake cookies, to do his homework—anything that might keep him indoors and prevent me from being alone with Dad. But when Dad caught on to this he nearly always managed to undermine my scheme, offering Andy something better if he left, or simply ordering him to do so.

Many Saturday mornings I tried to talk Mother out of going shopping.

"Do you *have* to go?" I'd ask.

"Yes, Kathy," she'd say, irritated by my question and my tone. "I have to get material for your new outfit. We need groceries, and there's a whole load of cleaning to pick up. Of course I have to go."

"Can I come with you?"

"Don't be silly. I can do it faster without you."

"Please, Mother," I'd plead, "I can help. I'll drive the car for you."

"I said *no*, Kathy. You've got plenty to do around here. Now get going."

Sometimes, when all else failed, I was very direct with Dad.

"K-K-K-Kaaaattttyyyy." His high-pitched voice called to me down the hall. "Where are you, girl?"

"I can't do it, Dad," I'd say when he appeared in my room, willing to endure his wrath, willing to sacrifice my privileges, disgusted by the thought of his body.

"You have to," he'd say, furious that I didn't need to negotiate for anything. "I need it. I don't get enough from your ma."

"I know you do, Dad. I hear you." And often I did, hoping it would get me off the hook, though it never seemed to.

"I need it more than she does, Katy. You gotta take care of me." He'd long ago abandoned any rationale except his own need.

"It's not right. It makes me feel too guilty."

"But I need you, Katy. I get so excited around you that I can't control myself."

"You could take care of yourself, you know," I suggested. "You could masturbate."

"Men don't do that," he scoffed, "only queers. I have to

have a woman, Katy. I need to be attracted to someone before I can make love with them, and I'm attracted to you. I want you. You gotta take care of me."

Most often I capitulated, getting it over with quickly, trying to put it out of my mind immediately afterward, purchasing peace, buying time.

And to deal with the residue of disgust this left behind, I turned more and more to my religion. Mother, passing on her family's creed, had taught me that it was legitimate to petition God and believe that He might respond. There were two catches, however: you had to have sufficient faith and your wish had to correspond to God's will.

I worked on my faith diligently, praying in church and out, walking around during the day and on my knees at night. I prayed that I would be forgiven for the incest and that it would cease. I read the Bible from beginning to end. I saved the sermons which our pastor preached and read and reread them. I began to collect Bibles: I had fifteen by the time I finished high school. Despite my shaky self-image, I tried to develop a belief in myself, feeding myself doses of dogma ("All things are possible through Christ who is our Lord"), listening over and over to music I found inspirational, uplifting, with "Climb Every Mountain" from *The Sound of Music* at the top of the list.

Despite my rigorous religious efforts, I didn't gain much relief from the sense of sickness and shame that lay just below my carefully manicured surface. I had to employ ever more sophisticated tricks to somehow absent myself during sex with Dad, to pretend I wasn't there, that it wasn't happening. I became adept at blurring reality, sometimes erasing it altogether, a skill it's been most difficult and painful to unlearn. I did this by transporting my mind to other times and places. Instead of being on my bed, lying pinned beneath my father's hands, I was a little girl meandering through Grandma Hinkle's pastures, smelling the tall grasses, listening to the mournful sounds of the cows. Or I was standing in the Hartland candy store, gazing at the tall jars of brightly colored sweets, trying to decide which I'd like best. Or I was racing down the stairs of the old farmhouse on Christmas morning and seeing the packages spilling out from under the tree, then opening them slowly one by one.

Dad, keeping up, began to develop new tactics to hook me. He used my relationship with Roger to gain additional sexual leverage.

"I know what you two are doing," he'd say to me. "Do you think I don't know? Just don't think you're getting away with anything."

The implication was clear: if you can do it with him, you can damn well do it with me, too. What's the difference?

The injustice of this made me furious. In fact, Roger and I were very chaste with each other. I hated Dad pushing his dirty thoughts onto us. To shut him up, I would comply. And once I'd decided to, my thought process was always the same: hurry up and get it over with; at least he'll be nicer, in a better mood; I'll forget it when it's over; I won't have to worry about it for a few days.

One Saturday in the winter of 1961 he unveiled another new approach. I was standing at his bedroom window, watching Andy disappear down the street. Dad was rummaging about in his closet.

"K-K-K-Kaaaattttyyyy." He sang out my name.

"Just a minute, Dad. I want to make sure Andy's gone."

"Oh, don't worry about him, girl. I gave him enough

(77)

money to last hours at the store. C'mon over here. I wanna show you something."

He was naked, sitting on the bed, holding a handful of photographs.

"I confiscated these," he said, relishing the use of this official word. "Took 'em away from the boys at the reformatory."

As I sat down on the bed, he spread out the pictures so that I could see them. They showed naked men, naked women, and animals in all sorts of sexual positions with each other. Looking at them, I felt a rush spread through my body, and once again the cycle was set in motion: intense sexual desire, total revulsion, increasing excitement, abandonment of reason, surge of climax, sense of sin and guilt and shame of it all, resolve to forget it until next time.

My public life went along quite smoothly during my junior year. The pose that I'd developed vis-à-vis my girlfriends—slightly apart, slightly superior—was working successfully. I was something of a pacesetter in the group, entitled to be a little different. After all, how many girls could shinny up a hundred-foot rope in gym, bat a baseball fifty yards, charm so many boys, get straight A's, have her own car, be elected to nine or ten organizations, and go steady with one of the neatest boys in school?

The only flaw in my relationship with Roger was that he seemed bent on keeping me apart from his family. They had no idea at this point that I even existed. I tried not to let this bother me, and when he spent every Friday night with his parents at their cottage, I made sure to have plans with my folks so that I wouldn't feel neglected.

Nearly every restaurant in Great Rapids featured a fish fry on Friday nights, competing with one another by advertising in the local paper their bargain prices and their long lists of "extras" to go with dinner. Each week Dad and I combed through the ads, deciding which restaurant was offering the most that week, presenting Mother with our choice when she arrived home from work. I think she may have wondered why I always had to be along; I think she may have been jealous that I was. But her capacity for pretending was almost as great as mine, so these feelings never showed.

I didn't suffer a moment of the usual teenage humiliation at being seen with one's parents. When we all went on weekend fishing and camping trips, I didn't wish to be home with the gang, despite the discomfort of having to deflect my father's sexual advances. My priority was still to perpetuate the illusion of the wholesome, happy family, and I attempted to play it out whenever I could.

Mother had given Dad a movie camera for Christmas in 1960, and I seized on home movies as an opportunity to set up scenes of affection between my parents, directing them to wrap their arms around each other, to kiss. I loved the Sundays when we went for drives in the afternoon, although Andy, who was only twelve, had already bowed out, finding these occasions boring, an embarrassment. No defiance or rebellion for me—I wanted *togetherness*, the appearance of intimacy with both my parents simultaneously.

Roger was uncertain of his plans for the future after he graduated from high school in June of 1961. His family would have been happy to have him skip college and go directly into Brady Industries, Inc., which owned several light-manufacturing plants in the area, a good portion of the real estate in downtown Great Rapids, a statewide system of grain storage warehouses, and some timberland up north. That would have pleased me, too, as it would have kept him in Great Rapids. He, however, decided that he needed to get away from home, that he wanted a college education.

His decision made me angry. It hurt my feelings. He was the main prop of my public persona, and I didn't know what I'd do without him.

Late in August, a few weeks before he was due to leave, he and his boyfriends got together for a farewell blast. That same night my girlfriends were having a beer party. I'd never participated in one of these before. As my father's sex partner, Ellen's sister, and Roger's girlfriend, I'd taken special pains to keep my reputation very straight. I had to protect myself against anything that could detract from my "nice girl" image. This night, however, I decided to go along—maybe because I was angry at Roger, perhaps to test him.

Congregating in Sheryl Persky's basement, we drank the beer rapidly, throwing empties against the walls and watching them bounce, laughing uproariously, telling tales on each other to the accompaniment of increasingly drunken giggles. I must have had about two six-packs by the time we decided we'd try to catch up with the boys at Bailey's, the local hangout. Driving there, I became very sick, holding my head out the window, hoping the air would stop it from spinning and settle my stomach. It didn't, and I ran for the ladies' room the moment we arrived. Apparently I passed out; I next remember hearing Roger's voice outside the door, trying to persuade a waitress to let him come in to get me. Succeeding, managing to get me into the car, he lectured me all the way home, reprimanding me for my tasteless behavior, pointing out its ugliness. Ashamed, guilty, I listened in silence, certain I deserved the rebuke.

When we arrived at my house Roger explained what had happened. Mother calmly accepted his story. Dad was enraged and didn't believe a word of it.

Naked to the waist, he wore pajama bottoms which clearly revealed the outline of his penis swaying, unrestrained, between his legs as he paced up and down the living room, flinging his arms and accusations about wildly.

"Do you think I'm an idiot? Do you think I can't see what you've been up to—filling her up with beer so you can do whatever you want to her? Well, you're not going to get away with it!"

Going to the phone, he called some cronies on the police force and requested they come to the house immediately.

When they arrived and heard the different versions of the evening, they obviously believed Roger and were as embarrassed by Dad as Mother and I were.

"Aren't you gonna do something with this boy?" Dad's face was red, his voice hoarse from yelling. "Teach him a lesson?"

"Look, Tom," one of the men began quietly, "it seems like the boy was just helping out—"

"Are you blind?" Dad screeched. "My girl's drunk, and you can bet this punk wasn't planning to help out anyone but himself! Now if you can't see that—"

"Please, Tom," Mother broke in, "just let it drop. There's nothing they can do."

Dad shot her a withering look.

"Maybe you ought to look to your own house, Tom,"

one of the policemen suggested softly as he and his partner made a hurried exit.

"What's that supposed to mean?" Dad hollered after them, standing half naked in the doorway.

"Get in here," Mother chided him. "Stop making a damn fool of yourself."

"Don't you tell me what to do," he thundered at her, turning back into the living room.

"And don't you think you're getting away with anything," he said to Roger, stabbing a finger at him before storming off to bed.

Mother tried to make excuses. Roger left as soon as possible. I sat, sodden, in one of the armchairs, saying nothing, feeling as though my life were over.

CHAPTER

7

"These recent looks into the past have brought out demons long hidden. Sometimes the past haunts me."

—*Andy*

I was desolate when Roger went off to college. Even with the barriers between us, I'd been close to him. He was my insulation against the ugly reality at home, and his absence made me feel acutely lonely, abandoned again. I wrote him often, expressing my need for him, anxiously awaiting his few return letters. They showed, quite clearly, that he was trying to maintain some distance from me.

I didn't call you when I was home because I did not want to interfere with anyone that was taking you out because I know how I would feel if I was in his shoes.

Like I once told you, there are many people in this world. I have gone out with just about a different

(83)

girl each weekend since I've been here and they seem to be a little more advanced than the general high school girl.

In regard to Thanksgiving do not hold back on my behalf because I will not have much time to really spend with you anyway.

I think if you stay active . . . you will find somebody that will love you and of course you can do the same in return.

Mother, suddenly sensitive to my situation, encouraged me not to give up on Roger, considering him a good catch. At the same time, she prodded me to become more involved in school activities as an antidote to my depression. More than ever now, without Roger to bolster my spectral sense of self-esteem, I needed proof that I was liked by large numbers of people. My amiable, animated, attractive facade, offensive to no one, acceptable to all, stood me in good stead. In October I was elected Color Day Queen and crowned at the first big dance of the fall semester.

Mother was ecstatic, participating fully in my moment in the spotlight, shopping with me for my outfit for the dance, interested in every detail of the preparations for the big day. Dad was resentful, jealous of the honor that took me away from him, refusing to show any pleasure.

"I don't see why you're making such a big thing of this, Lou," he complained often during the week preceding the dance.

"Oh, for God's sake, Tom," she answered him, "can't you at least let her have her day?"

"I just don't see why it's such a big deal," he insisted.

Mother attended the dance, leaning over the gymnasium balcony, grinning, taking an endless series of snapshots of me and Aaron Block, my date for the evening. Dad stayed home, and this hurt me terribly. I wanted to be able to look up into the balcony and see both of them sitting there, together, a normal mother and father come to celebrate proudly the achievement of a normal child.

Along with deflating my excitement over special occasions, Dad never missed a chance to point out Roger's shortcomings. When he was home for a weekend and Dad knew I was waiting around for the phone to ring, he taunted me relentlessly.

"Now I wonder who she's hoping to hear from?" he'd say, pretending confusion. "I wonder who's keeping her hanging around here, waiting and waiting? See how he's using you, that no-good playboy? He doesn't care about you."

Dad didn't care much for Aaron either, a frequent date of mine during my senior year. But the only thing he could really hold against him was that he was a Jew.

That was one of the things about Aaron I especially liked. He was the only Jew in the school, making him special. He was also smart, confident, gregarious, and president of the student council. He planned to go to Israel when he graduated. He said he'd like to take me with him.

I was charmed by Aaron's attention, fascinated by what I saw as his worldliness, awed by his profundity. At the same time, he was no real threat to my feelings for Roger, who remained elusive but still in touch.

"I ask myself," he wrote in one of his rare letters, "why

don't you tell her you're through, finished, washed up?
But I can't bring myself to the point to even begin."

I turned eighteen in December of 1961. Mother, typically, was away on my birthday, down-home visiting her
mother. Dad had planned a night on the town to celebrate
my attainment of legal age—an introduction to the local
watering holes.

We went to several places that night—the Golden
Horseshoe, Johnny's Eight Spot, the Candlelight Lounge,
the Embers—and all along the way Dad instructed me on
the safest way to drink. Although he didn't hold liquor
very well himself, he thought he had the answer: order
whiskey straight or with water and stay away from mixes
because they're what make you sick.

I followed his advice even though I didn't like any of
the drinks and even though it obviously wasn't keeping
him sober. He was becoming wobbly, his words a little
blurred.

At some of these places we danced, and as we did, his
arms around me much too tightly, he commented lewdly
and often on the women who danced past.

"I'll bet she's good in bed," he said of a tall, heavily
made-up blonde.

I tried to shush him, embarrassed to see my father leer-
ing at strange women, fearful that someone would over-
hear.

"Look at the tits on her," he noted of another.

I was uncomfortable and scared. I knew he was building
up to something, alluding to the empty house that awaited
us at the end of the evening, speaking with some urgency
about when we'd be alone.

At home, in bed, he urged me to have intercourse with

him. My resistance somewhat lowered by alcohol, and still, *still* wanting to please him, to make sure he'd love me, I tried.

"Do it this way, Katy," he said, his voice shaking with excitement as he guided my body onto his. "Your ma likes it this way, and you will too. Just go up and down, real slow, just up and down."

With his hands on my hips, he tried to pull me down onto his enormous penis, thrusting inward, upward. I felt it filling me, moving deeper inside. And I felt pain. It was too big. I was terrified.

"It hurts, Dad," I cried out, the little girl looking to her father for protection. "I don't want to do it."

"Okay, Katy, okay," he said, soothing, gentle. "You don't have to. We'll just do what you like."

What I *liked* at this point was what was quickest. What he liked was denying responsibility. If I'd completed intercourse with him, he would have rationalized that he was accommodating me. He never missed a chance to reinforce the idea that I was the initiator. And he did it very effectively. My sense of responsibility, the thing that bound me most forcefully to silence, was strong.

"Do you remember how you used to be?" he'd ask me. How was I? I'd wonder.

"Do you remember what a little tease you were?"

It was true. I had been. One piece clicked into place.

"Do you remember how you used to crawl in bed with me?"

Yes, I had done that. Another piece.

"You were such a little hot-pants . . . remember?"

I recalled my curiosity. My God, it was clear. I'd led him on, seduced him. I must have.

(87)

Christmas of 1961 was a typical Crosley family occasion, with all the usual currents running through it. Mother complained for days ahead of time about the amount of work required to make a big dinner. Dad used every complaint as an opportunity to take a swipe at Ellen and Bucky.

"It wouldn't be any big deal if we didn't have to have them," he said. "They just make a lot of extra work."

Although she basically thought the same thing, Mother couldn't stand to hear it. It sounded so un-Christian. A remark like this from Dad usually kept her quiet for a while.

I, of course, was busy trying to make everything nice, relieving Mother of as much of the work load as possible, trying to tease both Mother and Dad out of their respective discontents, enlisting Andy's help in decorating the house —no easy matter since he was now thirteen and disdainful of family affairs.

On Christmas morning Mother, Dad, Andy, and I opened our gifts to each other. Dad always made the biggest fuss over whatever I gave him. Ellen, Bucky, Evan, now two and a half, and their new baby daughter arrived around noon. Dad didn't even bother to get up from his rocker, mumbling a cursory greeting, returning immediately to the slow, undulating motion that seemed almost to hypnotize him. Mother gushed over them excessively in an effort to compensate. Ellen and Bucky bore both responses uneasily.

When Mother shooed them out of the kitchen they gladly retreated to a corner of the living room to play with one of Andy's new games. I flew from one place to another, helping Mother in the kitchen, playing adoring aunt with my niece and nephew, poking Dad whenever I passed him, trying to prod him out of his mood, taking Ellen into my room to show her my Christmas presents.

The meal itself was just like any other at our house. Mother babbled on and on about her job—the doctor was sloppy in his office procedures, the doctor was a poor diagnostician, the doctor was too abrupt with his patients— while we all rolled our eyes and Dad harped at her to leave the job if she found it so unsatisfactory.

After dinner Andy left immediately, going off to meet friends who'd escaped from their families; Dad and Bucky watched a football game on television, their only point of contact during the day; and Mother, Ellen, and I cleaned up.

I actually enjoyed a day like this. We were together, going through familial motions, and if you'd just seen the film, without the sound track, it might even have looked at moments as though we were having a good time. The surface was what was important to me. I couldn't afford to delve much deeper than that.

Remembering my Color Day triumph, when the time arrived in February for the election of senior-class officers I decided to run for president, this time stressing brains rather than beauty. I lost to Aaron but was elected class secretary, about the best a girl could expect to do in the early sixties. Shortly after that the local DeMolay chapter chose me as its representative in the state Sweetheart Contest. I didn't win that either, but being a candidate was reward enough. It told me I was okay, despite the dark fears hovering under the facade. In May I was prominently featured at the Honor Day Celebration, a rite recognizing students who'd achieved academic excellence.

Dad caviled at me on each of these occasions. He simply

hated me to do anything, have anything, enjoy anything, apart from him. When I did, he had to undermine it, by ridicule, innuendo, outright criticism. And his sexual appetite seemed only to increase as my aversion to him grew. He insisted, no matter what the circumstances.

"Oh, Katy, please take care of me. I need it real bad."

"No you don't," I'd whine in protest. "You and Mother did it last night. I heard you!"

"But I need more than most people. It's just the way I am."

Once, his teary pleas had elicited sympathy. The poor man, I'd thought. It must be awful to feel that way. Now I felt only repugnance, but still I'd submit. Hurry. Get it over with quickly.

He took greater and greater chances, risking discovery. On a fishing trip during the spring of my senior year he kept up a running stream of sexual suggestion.

"You look awful good to me in that swimming suit," he muttered when I passed near him.

"I'd sure like to get you alone, you little hot-pants," he whispered.

I was disturbed and repelled by his insinuations, but at least, I felt, I was protected against actual physical contact. The cabin was tiny; the fishing stream ran nearby; there was nothing resembling privacy. But on the final morning he cornered me in the cabin, cajoling, then begging, wrapping my hands around his erect penis, demanding.

I was appalled. My mother sat on a log no more than a hundred yards away, untangling fishline. She could come in at any time. She could probably even hear us where she was. Instinctively, I held my breath. The panic helped by filling my chest, making it difficult to get air. Don't make a sound. Hurry. Get it over with. I pumped my hands up and down. I've never been more frightened in my life. Still, I submitted.

Increasingly depressed by my powerlessness, I longed to tell someone of my dilemma, of my relationship with Dad, of what I was beginning to sense it was doing to me. I considered again telling Mother, but was so overwhelmed by guilt and shame that I quickly abandoned that possibility. She'd think I'd caused it. She'd think I was dirty, sick. She wouldn't love me if she knew.

Maybe I could tell the doctor in whose office I was going to work that summer. But he might go to my parents, open the whole thing up. I'd once longed for this. Now it terrified me. Mother would blame the trouble in the family on me. She wouldn't love me. She'd think I was dirty, sick.

What about our next-door neighbor, Mrs. Christianson? She was a sensitive woman, easy to talk to. No. I needed her approval. I wanted her respect.

Roger? Never. I couldn't risk losing him.

There was no safe way for me to get rid of the depression, the fear, the self-loathing. I just had to concentrate all the harder on my outer layer.

Going to the prom with Aaron was ideal in this respect: class president and class secretary, the perfect couple. It was even better than if Roger had come home to take me, as I'd hoped he might.

After the prom we changed out of our fancy clothes into sweaters and slacks and traveled twenty-five miles to the cottage of a classmate for an all-night party. Pleasantly high from several glasses of champagne, Aaron and I wandered away from the crowd to an upstairs bedroom and lay down together with our clothes on. We wrapped our arms around each other and began kissing.

"Take it off," he whispered a few minutes later, tugging at my sweater. "Take it off."

I could feel his hands trying to slide my sweater up over my head. I could feel his penis stiffening as he held me against him. I panicked, a picture of Roger filling my mind. I couldn't spoil myself with another man. I was saving myself for him.

I leaped up abruptly, much to Aaron's surprise and disappointment, and returned to the crowd below. I never thought of Dad, that I'd already been "spoiled" by him. My mental compartments were very clearly separated. Dad never entered my mind.

At the end of high school my thoughts of the future were clouded by apprehension and uncertainty. In a senior-year theme which pondered the topic "Commencement—The Beginning or the End?" I was quite brave, clucking over those schoolmates "who at the age of seventeen and eighteen think themselves quite capable of marriage," resolving for myself "to grasp the new rung on the ladder, for my new start in an ever more advanced society." Off the printed page I was not nearly so courageous.

Going away to college meant escape from my father. But it also meant that I might feel the same awful homesickness I suffered as a child when I was sent to stay with relatives. It meant I would again be far away from Roger, who had decided to discontinue college and return to Great Rapids to enter the family business. It meant that my sexual enslavement to my father would be exchanged for the financial bondage of his paying my tuition. When I thought of college I saw a large blank wall, enigmatic and formidable. The unknown petrified me, and I hated myself for my fear.

Forgetting the contempt I'd voiced for classmates who
were rushing into wedlock, I began by summer to see
marriage as the answer to my problems. I didn't want any
surprises. I wanted to know exactly what was going to
happen to me. With marriage, I'd know. I already knew the
rules. I'd been a surrogate wife for years. If I got married,
I'd be safe. Probably freedom wasn't all it was cracked up
to be anyway. Who said it was so great?

So I decided to attend an extension of the state university
part time and work part time in the doctor's office while
I waited for Roger to come around to the idea of marriage.
And I would continue living at home.

Dr. Evans, my employer, urged me to reconsider.

"You ought to go away to school, get out on your own,"
he told me.

I overheard Mrs. Christianson, our next-door neighbor,
telling Mother the same thing.

"She's too docile, too unassertive," she said. "It would
do her good to get away."

But I was hopelessly dependent, incapable of autonomous action, alarmed by what might lie beyond the bound-
aries of my home, my town. The best I could do was to
decide that one man must rescue me from the domination
of another.

My submissiveness, my docility, would have surprised
my classmates. They saw me very differently, as their
messages in my yearbook indicated.

I would like to wish you good luck in future years
even though you probably won't need too much luck
with your brains and personality.

I must close and give someone else a chance to tell you how wonderful, smart, fun, neat, beautiful, witty, and charming you are.

With your personality you're bound to go places in this world. You sure can make a lot of yourself with your "get up and go."

I devoted the summer of 1962, the summer following graduation, to pinning down Roger on the matter of our future together. Mother fully supported the view that he was the answer for me. I didn't expect any endorsement from Dad.

Roger hadn't done well at college. His family name was meaningless there; no special aura attached itself to him. He was just another student, a rather undistinguished one at that. He abhorred this sort of anonymity, and eventually he began to return to Great Rapids for weekends. There he was somebody; he had a clearly defined reputation. He was William Brady's son. It boosted his ego to come home, where his mother doted on him, his friends knew his worth, he was recognized. These weekend boosts carried him through the year, but he didn't have the stomach to return for another. The family business looked better than it had a year earlier. He told his father he was ready to join up.

His commitment to me came more slowly. Part of his reluctance was based on his family's certain disapproval. They felt he was too young to be tied down, he told me. They wanted him devoting his energies to learning the business, to being groomed as his father's successor, to establishing himself as a young man to be taken seriously. What he did not tell me, but I knew intuitively, was that they would not want him involved with someone of my dubious social stature. True, I had shone in high school, collecting nearly every honor imaginable, certifying my popularity over and over again. But popularity wasn't breeding. I had once lived on Asbury Road; I now lived on LaFontaine. My father was a prison guard; my mother was a nurse. My sister had left high school at fifteen to get married because she was pregnant. My mother still sewed some of my dresses, all her own clothes, the bulk of Dad's. I was inappropriate.

But I was also undaunted by Roger's resistance, and I gradually wore it down by being exactly what he wanted, even though I'd been born into the wrong family. I made myself irresistible. I took his word as gospel, never questioning his views, his opinions. I bolstered his vulnerable ego by acting as though he were the most important person in the world, as indeed he was in mine. I behaved with the sort of mannerly restraint he admired. I always appeared picture-perfect, well groomed, well dressed, sunny, glowing. When he became slightly more adventurous sexually —touching my breasts, asking me to touch him—I willingly went along without seeming too eager. I was, quite simply, ideal. And finally he saw it.

His proposal, if it can be called that, came on a Saturday afternoon in late August and was replete with conditions. He thought it might be a good idea, he said, if we were engaged. That way we'd know we were committed to each other and that we weren't to see other people. But we couldn't think about getting married yet. There was no point even to discussing it at this time. It was a long way off. Also, our engagement would have to be secret for the time being. He didn't want to upset his family.

My excitement wasn't dampened in the least by Roger's

terms. We were engaged! That was all that mattered. I had a future. So it wasn't college or a career—so what? I was going to get out, get away, have my own life, one in which I had no doubt I'd live happily ever after.

Roger dropped me off at the house before going home to have dinner with his family and change for our evening date. I felt absolutely gossamer moving through the still, oppressive air, buoyed up by hope and happiness. Floating down the hall toward my bedroom, I heard water gurgling out of the tub, signaling the end of a bath. Mother, as usual, was out. Dad would want something from me.

In my room I struck a prim, businesslike pose, hoping to deflect the demand. I sat at my desk, new reading glasses perched on the end of my nose, *Wall Street Journal* open before me to the stock page, which I checked daily since purchasing five shares of General Motors.

A creaking noise and the smell of Old Spice told me he'd opened the door. The odor, which I'd grown to hate, made me nauseous. I glanced over my shoulder. He was naked, his foggy blue eyes protruding from under lowered lids, his face suffused by a salacious flush, his penis upright and hard.

"Hey, K-K-K-Katy," he cooed, "whatcha doing?"

"Reading, Dad," I said curtly, turning back to my paper, settling my body into an even more serious position in my chair. "I have to read this so I can do my stock chart."

I felt him move across the room, out of the corner of my eye saw him settle onto the bed beside my chair. I continued staring at my paper, trying to look absorbed.

"You know I joined a stock club, don't you?" He was trying to be casual, as though it were the most natural thing in the world for him to be sitting wholly bare, with a fierce erection, on the edge of my bed.

"Yes, Dad." I'd prodded him into it, hoping it would give him an interest in something other than me and an increase in male companionship.

"There's a new stock out that might interest you. Me and the boys are going to buy it up. It's called the Syntex Company and it looks real good. They make a pill called a birth control pill. Do you know what that is, Katy?"

"Yes, Dad." Knowing how his mind worked, I wanted to get off this subject. "And please don't call me Katy. I'm too old for nicknames."

"I can't help it . . . you'll always be Katy to me. Anyway, I don't want you to get all grown-up and smart-alecky. Pretty soon you won't want me to talk to you at all."

"I just don't like that nickname anymore, Dad. It's embarrassing."

"I'll call you anything I want, girl." His voice hardened, losing its purr. "And don't you forget it."

I turned back to my paper, shifted my body another few degrees away from him.

"You oughta get some of that stock," he said after several beats of silence, rubbing his hands up and down his thighs. "It's going to be real big. Maybe you oughta get some of the pills, too. Then we could do more than we do."

His cackle scraped along my nerves. I was nauseated by his presence, his smell. Oh, how I hated him! Why did I just sit there?

He stood up, looming over me, his body quivering in anticipation. "How about taking care of me?" he said. "I need it real bad."

"No, Dad, I don't want to." My heart was thudding in

my ears, making my voice sound faint. "I don't want to do it ever again, and I'm not going to."

"What's the matter with you?" He was irritated by my defiance but not really taking me seriously.

"It's wrong, Dad. The whole thing's wrong and you know it and I just can't go on with it. Besides," I blurted, "I'm engaged now."

"Engaged!" He was stunned. "Who to?"

"To Roger."

"When did that happen?"

"This afternoon . . . and it's supposed to be a secret. But I want you to know because I can't go to bed with you anymore. I belong to someone else now."

"Take care of me just one more time," he implored me. "You see how bad I need it."

And indeed I could. It was pathetic: this huge man, naked, begging, tears of frustration spilling from his eyes.

"I can't," I said. "It makes me feel too guilty. I worry that we'll get caught. I worry that Roger will find out."

His mien of entreaty vanished in a sweep of panic. "Don't you ever tell him about us," he said urgently.

"Don't worry," I replied fervently. "He'd never understand. He'd think it was sick. He'd kill you."

"No one understands like we do, isn't that right, Katy?"

I understood nothing except that I wanted to shed this life and begin a new one where I'd be safe, respected, loved.

"I guess it's time I let you grow up," he said. "It'll be hard for me, but I guess you're old enough to know what you want. Katy, have you done it with him yet?"

"I refuse to discuss my sex life."

"If you haven't, we could practice. We could go all the way."

"No thanks, Dad," I said politely. "I can wait to do that with Roger."

"I'm going to miss you taking care of me, Kathy," he said, finally dropping my nickname. "Do you know that?"

I nodded. "Maybe now you can get closer to Mother," I suggested. "I think she'd like that."

"I don't know," he grumbled, slumping back down onto the bed. "Do you hate me?"

"No, Dad," I said weakly. "Of course not. Let's just forget about it."

"Okay," he agreed, "but promise me one thing. If you ever need me to take care of you, before you're married or after, you just let me know, okay?"

CHAPTER

8

"I wanted him to feel how you must have felt, alienated from your family, the one thing everyone should have to keep sane in this crazy mixed-up life."

—*Ellen*

Finally my father was willing to relinquish me. Something had taken precedence over his need for sexual gratification: ownership, custody of me by another man. That was something he could understand, however much he resented it.

And I, of course, had not been able to say no to him until I had alternative ownership to back up my refusal. My depression, fear, alienation, my *sickness,* weren't valid grounds. Only claiming possession by someone else gave me the necessary strength. I was too devalued, obeisant, to act in my own behalf with no motive besides self-interest. But officially becoming Roger's property was sufficient reason.

When I ended the sexual relationship with my father, I decided also to forget it. It was a grotesque recurring dream that was now over. Nothing would be served by dwelling on it. I was determined to obliterate it, to put it literally out of my mind. I simply wouldn't think of it. That I continued to live at home for four more years, subjected to my father as a constant reminder, made this an enormous task. But my repressive powers, developed and refined over the years, were so great by now that I almost brought it off. Seldom did the memory of incest filter through to my consciousness.

I adopted a way of relating to my father that was a natural outgrowth of the public persona I'd built up. Still eager to please and to avoid conflict, I was pleasant, accommodating in many ways, and unfailingly superficial. I was able at home, for the most part, to skim along with a sort of vapid amiability that made me virtually immune to anything authentic.

Dad found it difficult to have me under his roof but unavailable to him. He nagged at me constantly about almost everything; he made nasty remarks about me, about Roger, whenever an opening presented itself. He urged me to get on with marriage, insinuating that he knew everything about my sexual conduct with Roger, warning me I'd get into trouble if I kept it up. He brooded more than ever.

Now that I had Roger, I began to lose my appetite for mass approval, preferring to focus exclusively on him. Having too many people around confused me. I invariably wanted to please them all, a difficult and exhausting chore. Friends were draining, demanding, I decided. They asked questions. They took up time. They flirted with my boyfriend. Who needed them? I began to drift away from my high-school crowd.

The post-graduation regimen I'd decided on—attending

the state university's branch in Great Rapids and working part time for Dr. Evans—lasted about four months. I found school neither challenging nor interesting. In fact, it came to seem an impediment to the course I'd laid out for myself. Since I was going to get married anyway, I began to reason, it made more sense to quit school and part-time work and get a higher-paying job, saving my money for the marriage that was increasingly my only goal in life. I went to work as a clerk at Ellingham Tool & Die, the best money in town.

This was a severe comedown in some respects. From the glittering pinnacle of high-school society I'd traveled in a few short months to being just another mundane member of the working-class herd. I clung harder than ever to my reason for being in such a lowly position: saving money for my marriage to Roger. The other girls were there forever; I was just passing through. It didn't matter that I was temporarily caught in the monotony of clerical tasks or that I'd abandoned the promise of further education. I was convinced that my freedom lay in marriage and everything must go toward that end.

To set myself apart still further, and to create another persona to go with this new phase in my life, I began to make myself over entirely. I stopped eating sweets and nearly everything else that I really liked and lost weight for the first time in my life. I began selecting my wardrobe from the best shops in town, always wearing high heels, designer blouses, cashmere sweaters, and expensive wool slacks, never blue jeans. I went to the Merle Norman cosmetics studio in Minneapolis and learned how to do makeup. I practiced modulating my voice so that its tone was pleasing; I eliminated all swear and slang words from my vocabulary.

When Roger left for six months in the National Guard in the spring of 1963 my metamorphosis speeded up. I grew my hair out and wore it in a twist on top of my head with a bun in back. I practiced my posture before the mirror in my bedroom, which I had redecorated in several shades of purple. I began to wear my glasses even when I wasn't reading. And, in keeping with the slightly intellectual tone I thought they lent my appearance, I set up a reading program which I followed religiously. Each day I read three newspapers front to back; each week I read every word of several national magazines; at least once a day I read something spiritual; and I read part of a classic —*War and Peace, 1984, Crime and Punishment*—each night before going to sleep. I continued to lose weight.

My efforts at transformation required that I spend a great deal of time alone. With Roger away, I preferred this anyway. After work, I arrived home at about four-thirty, retreated to my room, remained there until dinner, "working" on myself, emerged for a strained meal with the family, and returned again to my room immediately afterward. I insisted on paying my parents the rent of one dollar per day. I felt this gave me the freedom to do whatever I pleased when I was at home.

Mother left me alone for the most part, assuming I was going through a phase, not inquiring too closely. Dad intruded on me constantly.

"I guess you're just in there mooning over that playboy," he'd say, commenting on my withdrawal. "Well, you're wasting your energy. Seems to me if he cared he'd write more often."

"I could charge you more, you know," he said whenever I delivered my rent to him. "But the only reason I'm even taking this is so you learn that you have to pay your way through life. Nobody gets a free ride."

Often I stayed in my room in the morning until it was time to go to work, skipping breakfast to avoid being subjected to Dad's remarks or the scene he played out with Andy nearly every day. He now smothered my brother with the sort of attention he'd once lavished on me. And Andy, who was always ill-humored in the morning, hated it.

"Oh, Anda-Panda," Dad crooned, pulling Andy's earlobe, rubbing his hands up and down Andy's back. "Are you still asleep? Are you ready to eat?"

"Dad, please." Andy pulled away, obviously annoyed.

"Whatsa matter, boy? Why're you so mad at your pa? I'm just trying to feed you. I don't want my baby boy going off hungry."

"I don't want to eat," Andy snarled.

"Of course you do. See what I cooked you, Anda-Panda . . . smoky links, just like you like 'em, just like your ma makes. You have a smoky link while I fix your cereal."

To shut Dad up, Andy went through the motions of eating something, and then escaped as soon as possible. Mother most often remained in bed until nine, so that she missed this, too.

Just before Roger was to finish National Guard training camp I wrote him to expect a surprise when I came to pick him up in Chicago. I'd kept the extent of my new image secret from him; I was excited to see his response to the new, sophisticated me. It was indeed a surprise for him. He didn't even recognize me at first. And when he did, he was angry that I'd dieted away the full-breasted girl he'd left behind. He said I was too skinny. He also hated my hair, saying it made me look like a middle-aged school-marm. I was crushed, but my devastation was eased some-what by the fact that I had my ally back. I wasn't alone anymore.

I also wasn't any closer to getting married than I had been the summer before. Our engagement was still a secret, Roger insisting on the subterfuge. His parents had great plans for him, he told me, and an early marriage was not included. We'd have to keep it quiet a while longer.

I also began to hear rumors that Roger's parents blamed me for his dropping out of college and that they did indeed feel I wasn't good enough for him. The longer Roger kept me and his parents apart, the more stock I put in these stories. Typically, though, I never asked him directly why I couldn't meet his folks. I never asked if the rumors were true. I just built up a silent store of resentment, as un-willing to make waves with Roger as I had been with my father.

Our life quickly settled into a fixed routine. We both worked hard during the week, seldom dating but talking each evening on the phone. On Friday nights the two of us went out to dinner, usually at a nearby Holiday Inn. Saturday nights we went to the movies or spent the even-ing with Ellen and Bucky, who were fast becoming our closest friends. They were awed by Roger's status in the community; their sense of his importance gave him an ego glow he didn't get from old friends, who were already be-ginning to drift away from Great Rapids and discover a larger world. Ellen and Bucky were comfortable for me also because they were my family. They didn't threaten me; they were no challenge. I rather gloried in the fact that I was the instrument of their social elevation. On Sunday afternoons Roger picked me up after I'd had lunch with my family and we took drives into the country or spent the day at Ellen and Bucky's. He always brought me home sooner than I wished. Terrible Sunday-night depressions continued to plague me, and I liked to postpone them as long as possible. And then a new week began with exactly the same pattern.

Our sexual contact now consisted of petting and quick jerk-offs for Roger. He never touched me. Nice boys didn't do that to nice girls. I also abstained from masturbation at this time, as part of my self-improvement program.

My Sunday-night depressions began to spill over into the week. I worried, fretted nonstop about myself: was my hair perfect, did I have too many cavities, were my clothes pretty, was I spotless, was I too fat, too dumb, would Roger ever give me a diamond ring?

Each Christmas I hoped, I prayed, for this gift that I wanted more than anything. Christmas of 1962 had passed with an assortment of nondescript presents. Christmas of 1963 brought a color television set. Finally, on Christmas Eve, 1964, it arrived, carried by Roger into the house in a brown paper bag, which he casually tossed under the Christmas tree. Inside the bag was a box wrapped with gold-and-silver-striped paper. Inside that was another, smaller box wrapped in red. Inside that was the ring— proof, to me, that our bond was irrevocable.

The next day, five years after we'd met, he introduced me to his parents. I was triumphant. I had captured him and, in the process, crossed class lines into the upper crust of Great Rapids society. My facade had once again carried the day.

Once I possessed the ring, planning the wedding became

my raison d'être. If ever a project was designed to make someone feel like a normal American girl, this was it. Mother and I worked on all the plans together, proof that we were close, a normal mother and daughter. She was thrilled by the match I'd made, reveling in it almost as much as I did. Dad was disgruntled and tried to ignore it as much as possible, labeling our excitement "goofy" and "foolish."

And I loved seeing his discomfort, thumbing my nose at his opinions, flashing my brilliant ring in his face, planning my future, which would exclude him entirely. Now I didn't need his approval. Now I was getting out. Now I could count the days until I'd never have to deal with him again.

I became a devotee of *Bride* magazine, reading each issue cover to cover, researching the occasion which I believed would give me my life. I planned my wedding by the book, organizing it with the care and precision of a military campaign. It occupied me completely. Not even Dad's sour attitude could spoil my happiness or diminish my expectations.

Once I possessed the diamond ring, I also gave myself permission to have intercourse with Roger. We were practically married, just one step short of it. He liked to do it, and why make waves? After all, there wasn't much involved in it for me anyway. He'd don a rubber, quickly thrust into me, quickly climax and withdraw. That I didn't experience an orgasm was something I rationalized away; that I received no pleasure made me feel less guilty.

I began to see by the end of 1965 that Roger was no more eager to get married than he had been to give me a ring. He no longer kept me apart from his family. In fact, I was now employed by Brady Industries, Inc., doing light book-keeping and correspondence. But he remained slippery about a wedding date, as busy dodging that as I was ignoring the signs that marriage with him might not be a panacea for me. I saw him throw terrible temper tantrums when things didn't go his way, and watched his mother hurry to soothe and placate him. I heard him abuse her, and other women, verbally. He was contemptuous, dismissive. When I thought once that I might be pregnant, he immediately changed toward me, withdrawing, whining, implying that I was on my own.

Each time I received a piece of evidence of his character, I destroyed it. My tools for distorting reality, or canceling it, were abundant, and I used them all. I wanted a marriage with this man. I wanted to be rescued from my present life. Nothing must get in my way.

Finally, fed up with his vagueness about a date, I risked an ultimatum. One night when we were parked in our usual spot near the outskirts of town, necking our way toward a fast release for Roger, I disengaged myself and refused to continue.

"I think you're just using me for sex," I protested, "and I don't like it. Either marry me or we're through."

Even though his face was shadowed, I could feel Roger's shock. He was used to deference, submission.

"When I look ahead, it's blank," I said, my voice quivering, nearly as surprised as he by my action. "I need to know where I'm going. I'm tired of you getting what you want and paying no attention to me."

Astonished by my anger and my firmness, Roger quickly, almost meekly, consented to name a date: July 23, 1966, four o'clock in the afternoon.

CHAPTER

9

"I hope you will go about your new life and be happy. Look at the future, not the past. I will do my best to stay out of your business."

—*Dad*

The wedding took place on a hot sunny Saturday. My elation was so great I hadn't room for any other feelings. Not only was I being married, I was being liberated. At last I would be free, at last I would be safe—states between which I saw no contradiction.

Even my father couldn't diminish my triumphant optimism. As I lay outside in the morning, sunbathing, he came to say good-bye to me, a farewell reeking with sexual overtones.

"I'm going to miss you, Katy," he said, his voice husky, "miss having you here. You were my little girl, you know."

I gave a noncommittal murmur, refusing to engage.

"I'm glad you're doing what you think will make you happy, and I hope it will, but I'll always be here. I want you to know that."

"Sure, Dad." I knew he was making an offer I didn't even want to think about.

"If you ever need me, I'll be here."

"Yes, Dad. Let's just forget it now." I turned lazily away from him, a counterpoint of animosity running beneath my casual tone. I'm getting away, it said, out of your house, out of your sight. You'll never get to me again. This is the final severance.

I'd thought beforehand of the ironic and awful symbolism of my father's *giving me away* at my wedding. Perhaps to mute this, I had both my parents walk me down the aisle, one on either side. As I moved along the white runner spread the length of the church, I felt I was literally becoming someone else. I began the walk as my old self; by the time I reached the altar I'd been transformed into a new person. I truly believed, simplistically, idiotically, that the wedding ceremony marked not only my union with Roger; it celebrated the end of fear, loneliness, depression. I felt like a princess at the reception, gliding through the crowd of friends and relatives, reveling in my moment, whisked away finally in a chariot, our new silver Thunderbird.

Roger's parents' wedding gift to us was a honeymoon trip to Acapulco. Prudent, serious, we elected instead to put the money in the bank to spend as needed on our new home. We traveled forty miles away to a new Howard Johnson's for our wedding night.

The enchantment I'd expected when we were at last alone together as man and wife was missing. Roger's entrances into my body felt as rough and unsatisfying as they had in the back seat of the car. An overabundance of champagne left me feeling fuzzy and with a dreadful taste in my mouth. When I eventually slept, I dreamed the room had been broken into and I'd been raped. Awakening in the morning, I found the room empty, Roger having gone for a solitary swim.

The sense of foreboding fluttering around my edges increased the next day when we picked up the schnauzer puppy that was Roger's wedding present to me and, immediately and obviously, my competition. It was rather like being presented with a baby the day after one's wedding. The new young life took precedence over everything. Roger lavished attention on the dog, inviting her to sleep in our bed.

I remained apprehensive during the week following the wedding, which we spent settling into our new home, a three-bedroom ranch at the edge of one of the town's elite suburbs. I expected our first experience of married life to be romantic, emotional, felicitous, in a way my old life never had been. I had fantasized playing house with Roger, and every part of the fantasy was magic because it was shared. I saw us gazing at each other over morning coffee, our eyes adoring; I saw us removing clothing from suitcases, arranging it in the drawers and closets of *our* bedroom, talking softly, lovingly; we uncrated furniture, delighting in deciding what should go where; we toasted each other at candlelit dinners; and always, stretched between us, was an exquisite sensual thread that sometimes pulled our bodies close together, left them connected even when they were far apart.

In fact, Roger was withdrawn, nervous. He seemed wholly unaware of my needs or my expectations, ill at ease with our intimate situation, eager only to get back to work. The truth was visible in that first week: dressing up in elegant clothes and repeating words to each other beneath the roof of a church had not altered us. He was he and I was I. Only our status was different. The magic simply hadn't occurred.

I wasn't prepared to accept and face this reality any more than any other in my life, looking at it only long enough to see how I might be responsible. Clearly, I must be doing something to cause his inattentive behavior. I was, I decided, expecting him to play house. As an ambitious young man, bent on being a millionaire by thirty-five, coveting the presidency of the company, work was his absolute priority. I would work very hard; then he would love me. That determined, I submerged my misgivings in an almost obsessive dedication to continous labor.

The days were all the same. Because Roger expected me to serve a plentiful three-course dinner each night shortly after we arrived home from work, I began to get up at six in the morning to prepare parts of the evening meal before leaving for the day. We were at Brady Industries' offices from nine in the morning until six at night. Usually, after dinner Roger returned to work while I caught up on the housekeeping, laundry, ironing. When he returned about ten I stopped whatever I was doing and accompanied him to bed, as he demanded.

He was often dissatisfied with the food I prepared, sometimes refusing to eat it and throwing it down the sink ("Don't ever serve this again," he'd say, "it's trash"), sometimes ridiculing it by calling it "slop." I'd smile apologetically, occasionally cry, vowing to do better.

His sexual requirements were just as stringent and one-sided. He liked what he so aptly called "quickies," direct, sharp lunges into my body, immediate release for him, faked orgasm for me, no foreplay, no tenderness afterward.

He never asked what I wanted. He told me instead.

"You just need to get screwed," he'd say. "You just need a quickie."

We didn't discuss sex. We just performed this limited, unsatisfactory act that had so little to do with sensuality or love. Once married, we didn't even kiss each other anymore. Physical affection didn't exist between us. But always I remembered the results of my mother's reputed sexual denial of my father, where it had led, and I made a vow: I would never say no to Roger.

One evening several months into our marriage, I was ironing one of Roger's countless white shirts, watching on television the obligatory torrid love scene in a romantic 1940s movie. Home early, he barged into the room and snapped off the set with a disparaging remark.

"Who does he think he is?" I said to myself—silently, of course. "My father?"

Yes, the signs, the similarities, were there: another authoritarian figure who completely governed my life, whom I couldn't refuse; another spoiled child needing, insisting upon, his own way. I did what I hoped would make Roger love me; I ended up feeling used. I had relinquished my right to say no. Before marriage Roger had sometimes seemed sensitive to my needs, willing to understand and respond to them. Now that I was captive, he paid them no attention. He sought to satisfy only himself, no matter the price for me.

As chilling, as awful as these realizations were, I managed to shove them aside. I had, after all, an arsenal of gimmicks to distort, mask, or obliterate whatever was real. Even so, that terrible empty feeling was back again and I couldn't shake it.

When Roger and I married I withdrew quite abruptly

from my parents, It was healthy to erase old dependencies, I said to myself. I was a wife now, not a daughter. I didn't care that I was being cruel.

I seldom called, almost never invited them to my house. When we did speak, I was always rushing, able to have only a cursory exchange, keeping myself as remote as possible. I kept this distance in part to minimize reminders of the past. I also enjoyed impressing upon them the busyness, the importance, of my life now that I was a Brady. In effect, I told them I didn't have time for them. Somewhat awed by my elevated social status themselves, they were reluctant to force themselves on me, wary, I'm sure, of the cool reception they'd most likely receive.

Immersed in the Bradys' world, performing as a member of the firm or as Roger's wife, accomplishing the duties each of those positions required of me, I kept my defenses intact. By myself, outside those structures of expectations, I disintegrated. Loneliness and uneasiness flooded in. I couldn't concentrate enough to read. I couldn't sit still to watch television. When Roger went off for two weeks of Army duty, I felt completely adrift, floating through the house, wondering where everyone had gone, wondering why I was so alone.

I called Mother and made a luncheon date with her, planning to take her to the country club, where she'd never been and where I'd automatically become a member upon my marriage. I was to pick her up at one o'clock. I began getting ready about eleven in the morning, showering, sitting in front of my mirror, doing my makeup, my hair. At one I was still dissatisfied with my appearance, unable to make it come out right no matter how long I fussed. I called Mother and canceled, making some weak excuse, unable to explain it to her, not really understanding it myself.

I decided I needed to become involved in more activities. Working longer hours, needlessly redoing household chores, wasn't enough. I began collecting furniture, enrolled in classes in interior design, signed up for music lessons, took Gretel, our dog, to obedience school, became more active in the church. Even the constant motion these activities demanded couldn't remove altogether the sense of vacancy, the sense that even now I still wasn't present in my life.

Roger's refusal to be at all demonstrative became more hurtful, more rejecting, each time it happened. He didn't just withdraw or turn away. He rebuffed me verbally as well.

"Don't," he'd say when I touched him. "Leave me alone."

This rebuke was of a piece with his other judgments about me: I was stupid, incompetent, I lacked good breeding, I was where I was only because of my marriage to him. To combat this, to protect myself, I decided to remove myself emotionally from him as he had done with me. Let him say and do what he liked; I wouldn't feel it. I wouldn't let myself need him. I would, once again, just go through the motions of life.

As far away as I'd kept my father, he sensed that something was wrong. When Roger was at Army summer camp shortly after our first anniversary, Dad dropped in on me, the sort of unexpected occurrence I'd tried very hard to discourage. Typically, his visit included some genuine concern and a generous dose of sexual innuendo.

"How are you doing, Kathy?" he asked me.

"Fine, Dad, just fine."

"I hardly ever get to talk to you alone." He gave that familiar, detestable giggle. I recoiled inside from the sound's implication. "I can't really talk to you when your ma's around, you know what I mean?"

"I know what you mean." I kept my voice cold, the door closed.

"Is Roger treating you all right?" Translated from his private code, this meant: Was I getting enough sex?

"Yes, Dad. Everything's perfect."

"I know you pretty well, Kathy. And even if you don't want to talk about it, I can tell you're not happy."

"Of course I'm happy." I must have sounded somewhat shrill as I protested too much. "I'm as happy as I can be."

"We don't see you much. Seems all you ever do is work."

"Things are going great at work. I'm working hard, but I like it."

"You never have more than two minutes for me and your ma when we do see you. You seem to be running from something. What is it?"

I laughed off his question, sweeping my arms outward in a grand gesture. "Why would I be running? Do you see anything we don't have?"

"How's your sex life?" He dropped the code altogether in an effort to get past my surface.

"God, don't you ever get off that subject?" I said, exasperated.

"Okay, don't tell me about it, but I'll keep asking. I need you just like I always did. Your ma's never enough for me. I just want to remind you that I'm around."

My emotional detachment kept me from screaming at him. "Thanks, Dad," I said derisively, "but no thanks."

"Well, I'm just checking. I know you and I want to be sure you're happy."

"Why wouldn't I be? I've got a new house, a new T-bird, all the money I need. Everything's great, just great."

There was really nothing more he could say. The facade appeared successful. If he'd pointed out that I itemized my happiness by externals, if he'd reiterated his sense of my discontent, I'd have protested. My denial mechanism governed my life.

My self, embryonic though it may have been, had now vanished entirely, subsumed in the role of Mrs. Roger Brady. I'd sheared off all the ragged edges, the pieces of me which didn't fit that mold, by disconnecting my emotional system, simply pulling the plug. I was a perfect upper-middle-class robot, a little stiff perhaps, a little forced, but Roger seemed to like me that way. I didn't require intimacy, and that left all our energies free for work, his consuming passion. It took a pitcher of martinis for us to loosen up enough to impersonate husband and wife, the gin making possible a semblance of conversation, the performance of sex. But neither of us examined that. Roger may never have noticed it. The moment I did, I covered it up. The truth was, quite simply, intolerable. This man, this life, was meant to be my salvation. I had waited five years for it. It was what I'd wanted. I must continue wanting it.

Sometimes I relaxed my vigilance and the light of reality flickered momentarily in my inner darkness. When Peggy Lee sang "Is That All There Is?" it felt like a personal anthem, my melancholy straining outward toward the words of the song. Sometimes, driving in the car, standing at the sink, sitting at my desk, a question flashed in my mind: how do I get out of this? I tried always to smother the question, never to answer it.

Most of the time I quite adroitly kept the truth at bay. Influences that might have disturbed me were minimized by Roger's clamping an ever tighter lid on my outside activities, strictures very reminiscent of my father's. I could attend my classes, but he didn't like me doing anything else without his permission, didn't approve of my forming new friendships. There was no such thing as true friends anyway, he said, again echoing Dad. People only wanted to freeload, to get from us what they could.

He didn't object to my activities at church—singing in the choir, teaching Sunday school, helping to organize an adult Christian education program—even though he was not a believer and strenuously fought accompanying me to services on Sunday morning. I needed this tableau—young husband and wife, side by side, in pew—to bolster my sense of normality. And I always bought my own propaganda. On those occasions when Roger did come with me, I believed we were what we appeared to be: a glowing young couple, united, loving.

Ellen and Bucky were still our only friends. We could call them up anytime and have instant companionship, buffers to absorb the tension, take up the slack. Times we spent together focused on big dinners and lots of drinks. As bored with her life as I was with mine, Ellen welcomed the diversion. And gradually she and I began to develop a relationship apart from our husbands.

For one thing, she began cleaning my house, and I paid her just as I would have a maid, inflating the rate slightly. She needed the money and I liked being able to give it to her. She'd had a hard time, I felt. She hadn't been as lucky as I. Of course, she wouldn't accept money outright, but letting her work for me, paying her for her labor, was a way to make reparations. And it allowed us to spend time together too, no small matter for two lonely people.

We also enrolled in a correspondence course in fiction writing, keeping it secret from Roger and Bucky. I had always wanted to write but been fearful of trying, keeping my attempts to scribbled notes which I squirreled away and never transformed into any sort of defined entity. Ellen was willing to try anything that might be a diversion, an escape from the terrible depressions which made her feel suicidal.

The course resulted in Ellen's sending a barrage of snippets to the "Life in These United States" department of *Reader's Digest* for about six months. It caused me to make lists of subjects I might be interested in. I did very little actual writing. It demanded a focus and an emotional connection which were beyond me.

Roger objected even to my friendship with Ellen. It was a display of independence, however minor, that he couldn't tolerate. If she and I went to the movies alone, I had to hurry home afterward, feeling exactly as I had racing to meet the midnight curfew set by my father. When Roger was away I'd sneak in lunches with Ellen, shopping sprees. If I got caught, I was reprimanded.

On a spring evening nearly three years after our marriage, the phone rang very late at night, summoning us to the hospital. Roger's parents had been in an automobile accident. It didn't look good.

At the emergency room, the eyes of the nurses and orderlies telegraphed the message silently before the doctor put it into words: "Roger, your father is dead."

The shock was terrible, Roger's remorse overwhelming. He'd never told his father that he loved him. He'd never made amends for the hurtful things he'd said and done. He could find no respite from his grief.

The accident also left his mother crippled, in a wheelchair. But Roger had a solution for that: we must move in with her, just for a while.

I knew instinctively that this would be disastrous. I knew it was a mistake for me, for my marriage.

"We just finished fixing things up," I protested, clinging desperately to this last shred of autonomy, *my* house. "It's our home. I know your mother's had a hard time, but we'll get her a nurse, make sure she has good care."

"You can stay here then," Roger answered me, "but I'm going." He packed a suitcase and left the house.

Fearful, panicky, I drove to my parents' and talked to my mother.

"Go ahead," she counseled me, "it'll only be for a couple of weeks."

Ignoring my instincts, following the course that would gain me maximum approval, I wavered only as long as it took to circle the block once. Then, obedient, compliant, I entered my mother-in-law's house, leaving me further away from my freedom, from possessing my own life, than I'd ever been.

CHAPTER

10

*"We do what we have to to stay alive, to stay
sane, and that is no doubt a struggle."*

—*Andy*

Roger had enthusiastically endorsed my cutting ties to my
parents. But he hadn't been willing to do the same with his.
We had to stay connected to them, he explained, because
of the business.

I'd always thought he was attached too closely to his
mother, a woman like me: submissive, compliant, a con-
ciliator. When his father died and he insisted we move in
with her, I felt he'd made a choice—her over me. Clearly,
her welfare took precedence over mine. Once again an
important person in my life had put me firmly in second
place. My mother hadn't been willing to choose me over
my father; Roger was not willing to choose me over his
mother. *Poor little Kathy.* I was awash in self-pity, utterly
miserable.

Roger, still in shock over losing his father, clung tighter

than ever to his mother, including her in everything we did, making any semblance of privacy impossible for us. Everything happened in front of her: discussion of personal matters, making plans for an evening, talking about business, deciding what to have for dinner, arguments. She was always *there,* his attentiveness toward her giving me daily evidence of my second-class status.

Every day was a trial, a test. I became an avid reader of Christian Appeal literature, which came to me through the mail. Included in it were thoughts for the day. Each morning I'd grasp at a new one, repeating it over and over in my head throughout the day, looking in it for the power to keep going. At the same time, I railed against the God who could have put me in my present position. What good had my years of belief done me? I was still being taken, used.

My relationship with Roger was becoming increasingly shadowy. In addition to all our old problems, I now resented our living arrangement, his deference to his mother, his inability to recognize or understand my resentment. I never verbalized this, of course, preferring instead to sulk in silence. We drifted by each other in his mother's house, miming marriage. For the most part, we were courteous and correct with each other.

But we must have heard the hollowness in our behavior, because we came up with an antidote to it: we would have a child. That would fill the void, give us a solid meeting ground. Hardly unique, it was the same foolish, irresponsible solution so many troubled marriages clutch at, somehow believing a new life in the house will turn the parents into new people. I bought it, again looking for magic.

Once pregnant, I felt no different. I was still living in

my mother-in-law's house, submerged in my mother-in-law's life. Carrying a life in my body that belonged only to Roger and to me didn't make me feel any less trapped. At the risk of making waves, alienating my mother-in-law, angering Roger, I began to speak up. We couldn't stay here forever; we had to have our own place. To silence me, Roger began work on the Brady showplace we'd always planned someday to build. Just as I'd once counted on marriage for liberation, I now fixed on the house. When I had it, when we were living there, I would be free. I couldn't see that I was just digging myself in deeper and deeper.

When Roger entered the hospital room after the birth of Emily in mid-August, 1970, I knew immediately that he was jealous. Seeing her nursing at my breast, he instinctively moved away, petulance playing around his mouth. Then, finally turning back to me, he said, "You know, someday it's going to be just you and me. Remember that." However low his regard for me, he couldn't bear that I had to be shared.

Now that our child was present—the answer, we hoped, to our unhappiness—Roger seldom missed a chance to minimize her importance. He made it clear he didn't approve of my taking off too much time from work in connection with Emily's birth. He didn't feel it was necessary. Having a baby was no big deal, as he put it. I should be able to do that and work also

"You know, Kathy," he said to me, "there are countries where pregnant women walk in the fields behind the plows, and when the time comes, they lay the plow on the ground, squat down and give birth, and return to the plow."

He never helped in any way to take care of Emily.

Diaper changes and feeding times made him sick. He showed no inclination even to learn about the less offensive parts of baby care. He considered the whole thing my "problem."

He was worried and fretful about the new house. To be built on three waterfront acres in the country, it would cost several hundred thousand dollars, an amount that scared Roger. Maybe we couldn't afford it. Maybe we'd gotten in too deep. Still keenly feeling his father's absence, afraid of the responsibility it pressed on him, he complained endlessly, worked more obsessively than ever. I couldn't help him with his problems any more than he could assist me with mine. I didn't like hearing about his doubts and fears. He was supposed to be strong, to know what he was doing. After all, I'd put him in charge of my life—he'd damn well better know! Any whiff of weakness reminded me of my father, begging, pleading, needy, and these memories were insufferable. If these men, these authorities, were going to dominate my life, let them at least do it with conviction.

Finally located in our grand new house, by the spring of 1971, Roger's indignant, wounded mother left behind, I settled down to tending my new home and my new child. Both tasks absorbed me, and I felt relatively content. Roger was not pleased, however.

"You're getting lazy," he said one morning before leaving for work, waggling a parental finger in my face. "I think you'd better get back to work. Nobody in this family gets to just lie around. You'd better decide what your contribution's going to be to keeping this place going, especially if you want all the expensive trimmings."

I decided. I'd become a real estate broker, licensed by

the state, a license that would belong to me. But no sooner had I settled on something that contained a kernel of independence than I annihilated it by agreeing to become a subsidiary of Brady Industries. My firm was named for me, Katherine Brady Realty, Inc. Articles in the paper announcing its opening identified me as the second woman in the area to operate my own real estate company. But in fact *my* company was part of the Brady family conglomerate. My earnings were turned back to the corporation. I received only expenses and the "gift" of a beautiful Mercedes sedan to which the corporation held title.

The company did, however, allow me some margin in which to make autonomous business decisions, and I made good ones. The firm prospered and my slender store of self-esteem began to grow. I became wholly absorbed by this area of life, which allowed me to see concrete achievement. Two weeks after my firm opened, I became pregnant with our second child. I worked up until the day before her birth. Two weeks after Julia was born, I returned to work.

Roger viewed my new career with great ambivalence. He was proud of me; I was a feather in his cap. He was also jealous, and never tired of reminding me that the basis of my success was his family.

"You were nothing until you married me," he'd say. "The only reason you're getting listings and making sales is because you're a Brady."

But even this attitude couldn't completely undermine the new power I felt in myself. Let him take credit for my accomplishments, I decided. At least there were some. Perhaps I wasn't as unintelligent, as incompetent, as he'd always said, as I'd always believed.

My working did not mean that Roger demanded any less of me as a wife and mother. When he arrived home at night I was still expected to be there with a three-course meal waiting to be served. He complained terribly when I worked at night, on weekends, on holidays. He urged me sometimes just to let the phone ring, to forgo making appointments. At the same time, he criticized me for not making enough money. There was no way for me to win with him.

Our children were the bright spot in this rather bleak landscape. Emily, a delicate, winsome blonde with dark eyes, looked very much like Roger and at an early age demonstrated that she also possessed his stubbornness. When she decided on something, she could not be budged. Julia was round-faced, had bright red curly hair, and never stopped moving.

Once they were past the baby stage which he found so difficult, Roger began to pay attention to both girls, always slightly favoring Emily, whose pensive, passive manner was more agreeable to him than Julia's athletic one. He liked to play games and often spent hours at a time enchanting his daughters with amusements he'd devised. He sometimes stayed with them in the swimming pool behind the house for an entire afternoon. He always talked softly to them and treated them with gentleness.

When the children witnessed the arguments that occurred more and more frequently between Roger and me, their reactions reflected their personalities. Our clashes often took place at the dinner table, the only time of day we consistently spent together. Emily usually leaped in to play mediator, trying to smooth things over, to make peace. Then, later, she'd withdraw and I'd find her brooding in her room, puzzling over why her mother and father couldn't get along. Julia used the occasion of our quarrels to throw her food around, making Roger even more upset and angry. He reacted to her at these times much as my father had toward me when I was four and five years old. Afterward, Julia escaped into compulsive action, running about in the yard, climbing on top of cupboards, a whirling dervish.

The first time the word "divorce" ever even entered my consciousness was, ironically, on Mother's Day of 1975. Roger had been threatening to get a Labrador puppy, an addition to the household I was adamantly against. Nevertheless, with both our families gathered at our house that day, he appeared with the puppy and the protective armor of a dozen red roses, presenting both to me simultaneously. Throwing the roses down on the ground, I screamed at him, a most uncharacteristic action for me.

"You don't hear me," I said. "You don't respect me. It doesn't matter to you what I want or don't want."

Later in the backyard, speaking alone to my mother and his, I said: "This is it. I've had every insult I can stand. I'm going to divorce him."

It was the first time I thought, or uttered, the word. I quickly buried it, of course, but still, I had said it.

Our marriage, already impossibly strained, received another blow when I began to notice a decreasing sexual desire for Roger. It baffled me at first. Why wouldn't I want sex with him? I had finally learned to have orgasms within the abbreviated context of "quickies." True, I would have preferred more foreplay, more emotional reassurance. But it was better than it had been; maybe it would get better still. What was bothering me? Why didn't I want to?

Slowly, agonizingly, I began to comprehend why. "It'll just take twenty minutes," he'd say. "I've got to have it." I would start to demur, to stall. "You have no right to say no," he'd say. "You can't get out of it." His words reverberated noisily in my head, jarring loose pieces of the past. *You gotta help me, Katy. I need it real bad. If you don't take care of me I don't know what I'll do.* The disgrace I'd worked so hard to bury had surfaced. When Roger came toward me, I saw my father's face. When he spoke, I heard my father's words. The shame I'd put away forever had not disintegrated in the silence. Instead, it had grown, become swollen, distended, until finally it bobbed up, larger than ever.

Frightened by this specter and the feelings it provoked, I told Roger I was confused, that I needed to sort things out. I asked him to give me some time free of sexual demands, a request that led us into the first sexual discussion of our marriage. He had a problem with premature ejaculation, he admitted. I said I needed more time to climax. He'd always wanted more sexually than we had; now he wanted to try to learn. I had wanted more too; now I didn't know what I felt. We both agreed we needed counseling.

We took a course in transactional analysis. We sought traditional marriage counseling. We considered attending the Masters and Johnson sex clinic. In all of this I never talked about my father, but he was always there, now in the front of my mind. I knew there was a connection between him and what I was feeling.

The time came when we had to decide whether to pursue therapy at the Masters and Johnson clinic. To make therapy effective, I read, one should have a deep commitment to one's mate, a sincere desire to spend a lifetime with him. I realized that kind of commitment was now beyond me. I told Roger what I felt.

"I don't want to learn how to touch you," I said, "and I don't want you to learn how to touch me."

"Why didn't you tell me sooner about the things that bothered you?" he whimpered, frightened now by my revelation.

"Would it have mattered? It never occurred to you to ask."

I looked at his long face, filled with need, with feelings of rejection, and another wave of time past broke over me. It was my fault that he'd been reduced to such an abject state; it was my responsibility to rescue him from it. Just as I'd *taken care* of my father, so now I should *take care* of him. But I couldn't. The anger I'd been storing up for years intervened. His sudden attention to my sexual needs seemed as self-serving as his neglect of them had been. Now that he was scared, now that he thought I might leave him, he was willing to hear from me.

But I couldn't forget the verbal abuse: *you're dumb . . . you're stupid . . . you're no good . . . you're only what I made you by marrying you . . . the only reason you have anything is because you're a Brady.* I couldn't forget his coldness. Feeling frightened, pushed beyond my limits, I decided to take a break from the business world into which he'd pushed me. I wanted more time with my children; I wanted to stop running long enough to assess myself. He had no understanding to give me. "I knew all along you couldn't handle it" was what he said. I couldn't forget the humiliations, the opportunities he took to emphasize my powerlessness. Soon after I declared my sabbatical from the firm, Roger emptied the Mercedes and delivered it to a dealer to be sold. The father giveth and the father taketh away. *You have nothing on your own; you have only what I choose to give you.*

I said I needed time to think, time apart from him. I asked him to leave the house. Counseling had unveiled the differences between us but it hadn't resolved any of them. It had only revealed how insurmountable they were. More and more I saw how like my father Roger was. I now felt the same revulsion for him I'd felt for Dad years before. The years of Roger and I not hearing, seeing, talking to each other seemed to have left irreversible damage. He hadn't asked and I hadn't said. Now it seemed too late.

But it was frightening to be alone. When he called after four days and asked to talk to me, I agreed. He pleaded his case. I listened.

"If you want to come back, things will have to change," I said finally, outlining what I had in mind: more help from him around the house, an effort to see my point of view on things, an end to his insistence that I perform like Superwoman, no sex-on-demand.

In each instance he gave an absolute promise. Back in the house only a few weeks, he broke them all.

"It's not that I can't change," he said to me. "I'm just not going to."

Things were worse, not better. I told him I thought we should separate. Lying in bed one morning, he was keening with desire, pleading with me to work things out. I was overcome with a sense of *déjà vu.*

"I need you, Kitty," he said. "You mustn't go. Please don't leave me."

My God, I thought, it's just like Dad. It sounds the same; it feels the same.

"I need you," he repeated, pulling me against him so I could feel his erection. "I want you."

"This is no time for sex," I shrieked. "Can't you see I'm about to have a nervous breakdown?"

A few days later he woke me at three in the morning, demanding that we talk, insisting that we get up and go downstairs so the children wouldn't hear us.

"I want you to see a shrink," he announced. "If you don't, I'll have you committed."

He was saying it was my fault that we had problems. He was saying it was my responsibility to solve them. He was threatening to do something terrible to me if I didn't. My fault—"You remember what a little tease you were; you know you liked it." My responsibility—"You gotta take care of me, Katy; your ma just can't give me enough." His threat—"I need it real bad; if you don't take care of me I don't know what I'll do."

That finished it for me. I went to see my lawyer. A few days later I asked Roger to sit down with me at the dining-room table. The snow falling gently in large flakes outside the window accentuated the silence I felt inside myself, the silence of death, of loss.

"The divorce papers will be ready tomorrow, Roger. The sheriff will serve them to you at your attorney's office."

He stared at me, completely still, unspeaking.

"I can't live with you," I said, "and I don't want to add another ten years to our marriage trying to."

"I thought you were kidding about this divorce thing," he said, finally finding his voice.

"I know. That's one of the problems. You've never taken me seriously, as a human being, as a business partner, as anything."

"Your parents did this to you," he sputtered. "I've tried to change you but it doesn't work. You're no damn good."

"I know I can't change you," I said. "I can only change myself, but you won't allow it."

"What about the children?" he asked as their playful voices drifted up from the basement.

"Any life would be better for them than this one," I replied. "All they hear is business talk and arguments. Also, I'd like them to respect me. I don't see how they could, watching me live completely on your terms."

Roger rose and approached my chair, bending down to wrap his arms around me in an awkward embrace.

"Please, just leave me alone." I echoed the line he'd used so often in the early years of our marriage.

He moved away from me, uncertain what to do, no longer in charge, feeling his impotence. I watched him, unable to help, my own sorrow acute.

"When should I leave?" he asked quietly.

"I want you to go by this afternoon," I answered, just as softly.

He walked away and disappeared upstairs. It's over, I thought, gazing out at the soothing snow. It's finally over. I felt relieved, bereft—and very frightened.

I followed Roger upstairs. He stood in the bathroom, his back to the door, his face, made nearly unrecognizable by the contortions of sobbing, reflected in the mirror. The only other time I'd seen him cry like that was at his father's funeral. He turned and closed the door so I wouldn't see him. I moved back downstairs and lay on the living-room sofa, listening to the sound of him packing above me. After a time I heard his feet travel to the basement, where he explained to the children that he was going to stay with Grandma for a while.

Emily came tearing across the living room toward me. "Daddy won't ever put me to bed again!" she screamed, hurling her body on top of mine. Julia followed, imitating her sister even though she didn't understand. We huddled there together, listening as Roger loaded the car, started the engine, raised the garage door by remote control. Then I heard a horn and went to the window to peer out. I saw his familiar silhouette behind the wheel, and he waved at me, a bizarre and baffling gesture. Then he drove off. It was over.

Turning back toward the living room, I saw him lying on the sofa reading the paper. In the dining room he was sitting in his chair at the head of the table. I heard his voice and felt his presence in every room as I wandered through the house, despairing, dismayed by what I'd done. Upstairs, on the dresser in our bedroom, I found a note.

"Kitty," it said, "love our children with all your heart. Good-bye. Love, Roger."

I knew I'd done the right thing, made the correct decision, but I couldn't feel it then. All I felt was alone. Alone and apprehensive, and acutely uncertain.

And I felt that way for the better part of the next year, while I awaited our divorce. Roger staged repeated reconciliation attempts, his strongest argument based on our love for our children, the one positive thing we shared, his weakest, and most disparaging, that he'd be damaged by having his finances made public in a divorce proceeding. Occasionally I found his urgings persuasive. Occasionally I felt willing to do anything to eliminate the sense of loneliness and responsibility that bore down on me. But I knew instinctively that if we reconciled I'd lose myself entirely and irretrievably. I stuck to my decision.

My parents disapproved of the separation, believing strongly that my place was with my husband. When the first rumbles of trouble began, Roger had gone to them to solicit their help, line up their support.

"There's something wrong with her," he told them. "I think she's crazy. I don't understand what she's doing."

And neither did they. When we separated, they were shocked.

"What have you done wrong?" they asked me. "It's your duty to take care of him. You belong with him."

My resentment was ferocious. Wouldn't I ever come first? Was I now taking second place to Roger?

"I'm your daughter," I pointed out, fighting back. "He's only your son-in-law. Your loyalty belongs with me."

They knuckled under and switched it back, but only grudgingly, announcing they would not now be as available to help out with the children as they had been.

"It was one thing when you and Roger needed time to get away," they said, recalling how they'd kept the children while we'd gone on skiing trips, traveled to business conventions, taken holidays in Acapulco and Caracas. "But now we think your place is with your children. Because of your decision they are your burden, and you'd better learn to cope with that."

Their attitude was insulting as well as punitive. It couldn't have been clearer. I, by myself, did not warrant assistance. I just wasn't important enough.

The self-examination set off by the tumult in my life was agonizing. I'd attempt to take stock, then stop abruptly when I found the storehouse so pathetically bare. The only things I was sure I possessed were anger, loneliness, depression, confusion. I was out of my marriage but I still felt trapped. Once again, there was no magic. What was wrong with me?

One day, when I knew my mother was away, I phoned my father, breaking my vow never to discuss sex with him again.

"Do you remember the relationship we once had?" I asked him.

"I sure do, girl," he replied, his voice animated by excitement.

"I want to discuss it sometime," I told him, ignoring his tone. "Could we do that?"

He quickly agreed and rushed over to my house.

"I hoped you'd want to talk about this sometime," he said, intoxicated by my invitation. "I never brought it up when Roger was around because I figured you didn't need me. I'm avaliable anytime, you know. I told you that once, but I guess you forgot."

I was dumbstruck, horrified by what I'd unleashed. "No," I started to protest, "I didn't forget . . ."

"You know how I feel about you, Katy," he crooned. "Why, I could take up right where we left off."

"No, Dad."

His momentum carried him past my words, unhearing. "I know you're having a bad time now, being alone and all, and you know your ma is never enough for me. I'd like to take care of you again, Katy."

"No thank you, Dad." I drove the words into his reverie, puncturing it. "I want to tell you, as an adult, that there will never be anything sexual between us again."

His face fell, taking on the woebegone cast I remembered so well.

"As far as I'm concerned," I continued, "what we did was

wrong, and I wanted to talk to you so I could tell you that."

"Aw, Katy," he said, "I never meant—"

"Also," I broke in on him, "I want to make sure that you don't try anything with my little girls."

He yelped as though I'd slapped him. "How could you even think such a thing? I love those two as if they were my own. I'd never do anything to hurt them."

"I was your own and you hurt me. Why wouldn't you do it again?"

"It was different with you and me, special." His voice softened. "We were real close. You know how I feel about you. Well, I feel the same way about your kids. It's like you're all mine."

"That's what worries me," I hollered, enraged that he couldn't, or wouldn't, get the point. "They aren't yours, and neither am I. I'm an adult with my own life, and the kids belong to me and Roger."

"I know that," he whined.

"I don't want them ever to experience what I went through with you," I said. "And if you ever lay a hand on them, I'll prosecute."

His chagrin disappeared in a flash of anger. "Oh, you think you're so smart," he said in his prison guard's voice, "kicking your husband out so you can do as you please. Well, I'm on to you. I know what you're up to."

"The same goes for you," I retorted. "I want you to know I'm watching you with my kids. And as far as what I do with my personal life, it's none of your damned business. Guess whatever you like. I don't care."

"You don't fool me now and you never did." His face was flushed with aggravation. "You always were a little tease and you always will be. How do you think we ended up together in bed in the first place?"

That silenced me, as it always had. No matter how much time passed, the guilt was there, waiting. And he could summon it with ease.

"Let's not talk about it anymore, Dad," I said.

"Okay, Katy," he said, suddenly agreeable.

"I have things to do."

"Okay, okay . . . I'm out the door. But you let me know if you change your mind. I'll be around and I'll be ready. You just let me know."

CHAPTER

11

"What we are, do, certainly involves conscious choice. But so much is a culmination of circumstance and chance."

—*Andy*

During the last few years of my marriage I began paying attention to articles in newspapers and magazines about the women's movement. Its concerns seemed to mirror mine. I certainly had felt the inequity of being a woman in the business world, even though my employer was my husband's family. I knew the additional satisfaction I'd gained from defining myself as more than wife-mother. I'd experienced the frustration of being mired in a rigidly traditional marriage with my husband in charge of all the decisions. I read more; I talked to Mother and Ellen about my feelings.

"Kathy, you sound like a women's libber," Mother said, obviously finding the notion ridiculous.

"Maybe I am," I replied.

"Oh, nonsense! Those women are dissatisfied and frustrated. You have everything you want."

Ellen took a different approach.

"Why stir things up?" she asked me. "I remember a few years ago telling Bucky how unhappy I was and he acted like he didn't even hear me. I'd already spent ten years with him; I figured I might as well spend ten more. My life's over anyway."

I didn't bother trying to talk to Roger. He considered even popular self-help books—*How to Be Your Own Best Friend, Your Perfect Right, Born to Win*—subversive.

"I don't want you reading that stuff," he said.

So I didn't when he was around. I hid the books, pulling them out only when he left the house, sometimes taking one with me to work and stopping along the way on a back road to read for fifteen minutes or half an hour.

The reading made me feel hopeful and less alone. It also made me begin to see that perhaps I could effect changes in my own life. It gave me enough determination to sign up for an assertiveness-training course despite Roger's protestations.

"I don't care what they call it," he said. "What they're going to teach you is to be tough and pushy. Is that what you want?"

I didn't bother to argue; I just enrolled.

Angela, the woman who taught the course, impressed me enormously. She was articulate, self-confident, quietly powerful, things I was not but fervently wished to be. When the course ended, she stayed in my mind. I carried with me the image of her warm brown eyes, her open face framed softly by tousled dark hair. I heard her voice asking questions that made me think. I wanted to see her again. I knew she did private counseling, and I made an appointment to ask her to become my therapist.

Waiting outside her office, I was shaky, damp with

perspiration, but unaware of the source of my discomfort. Entering, seeing her seated behind a large mahogany desk, I thought how beautiful she looked. She poured me a cup of coffee, seated me on a soft leather sofa, returned to her desk.

"How are you feeling?" she asked.

Even her mellow voice didn't quiet my quaking, and I feared the coffee would splash over the side of the cup.

"Scared," I blurted.

"What's going on with you?"

"I'm confused." I managed to lower my quivering cup onto a small table, only spilling a little.

"Tell me about it."

"I can't." I could barely expel those words, pushing them past the obstruction in my throat.

"Is it because you care for me?"

Of course. Only when she said it did I know. "Yes." The word issued in a burst of surprise.

She stood up and moved away from the desk, toward the sofa, coming to sit beside me.

"Look"—she rested a hand gently on my knee—"I want you to know that it's okay for you to care for me. You can still tell me your problems."

Her words, her touch, reassured me. "I'm tied up in knots," I confessed. "I can't make love with Roger. I don't want him to touch me."

She nodded as though she knew what I meant. Perhaps she'd felt the same thing? Her own marriage wasn't good, she told me. There were four children, many problems.

"I'm committed to staying together for the kids," she said. "Barry and I share what we can share."

"That's not enough for you!" I surprised myself, and

her, with this eruption. "You're a wonderful person. It's not fair for you just to exist."

"Fair? Nothing's fair. Where is it written that life's going to be fair?"

"I don't know," I murmured, embarrassed that I'd overstepped my bounds, revealed my ignorance.

She began to talk then of another inequity in her life. She'd had an affair with a priest, was perhaps still in love with him. They seldom saw each other, now almost never. As I watched her talk, something moved inside me, stirred, then churned, reddening my face, warming my body.

"We've finished our fifty minutes," I heard her say, penetrating my haze of excitement. "Next week I'll be in Chicago at a convention, so let's talk again in two weeks."

She returned to the desk, wrote out a bill for me, searched for a piece of literature she wanted me to read. I stared intently at her, recording every move, memorizing the essence of her face and body, pictures I'd take with me so that I could pull them out later for solitary scrutiny.

When I reached the doorway she joined me there, hugging me against her affectionately, setting off a thudding in my ears that muffled her good-bye. I floated to my car, feeling expectant, energized.

Each session I had with Angela increased my attraction to her. At first I was appalled. Was I one of *them,* I wondered. Probably, I decided. Quite quickly my shock vanished in euphoria. Why should I deny these feelings? They felt so good; they'd been absent so long. This time I *had* found the magic, the way to self-discovery, freedom. What I didn't see was that I'd just found another candidate for president of my life.

During each session I also tightened the restrictions I

put on myself. I wanted to talk about the incest, to discover why it kept pushing into my mind, haunting me. But I couldn't. It might disgust her, destroy her respect for me. I couldn't take the chance. I also couldn't go any further in therapy while I was avoiding it. I decided I'd have to discontinue treatment, a decision that left me desolate. The threat of losing her was awful. The threat of the incest being revealed was worse.

The day I told her I couldn't continue I also admitted my sexual feelings for her. I needn't worry about being abandoned, she assured me. We could maintain a relationship as "friends."

The promise of this alliance led me into an orgy of ingratiation. Shortly after Roger and I separated, I took her on a skiing trip to Aspen, all expenses paid. There, in effect, I pimped for her.

"You're better at talking to people than I am," she said. "See if those two guys will have a drink with us. You'll know what to say."

"You want them? I'll get them," I boasted. And I did.

During that trip she hit on the idea that what our town needed was a feminist bookstore. I leaped to commit myself to being a full-paying partner. I remember thinking: I'll do anything for her that she wants.

I paid for the apartment she kept in a nearby university town where she was taking courses. I chauffeured her there in my car a few times each week, and anywhere else she wanted to go. I immersed her in a steady stream of gifts— flowers, clothing, jewelry, poetry of my own making— and regularly proffered my body as well. It was the only offering of mine she ever refused.

The pattern was repeating again. I was wholly dependent upon her, looking to her for all my answers, severing connections with Ellen and Mother, isolating myself in the cocoon of my infatuation. Once again I focused on an authority figure to whom I handed over control of my life, unable to say no to anything she might want, willing to go to any length to avoid rejection, assuming the tune she was calling was correct. This time the currency was different— I bought her with money, goods, services, not with sex— but the transaction was essentially the same.

The pain of unrequited love was terrific, yet I couldn't move away from her. I was mired in a kind of hopeless dependence, my well-being rising and falling on the smallest indications of pleasure or displeasure from her. I'd beg to sleep with her—not to have sex, just to spend the night in the same bed. If she agreed, which she sometimes did, life was worth living. If she did not, a more frequent occurrence, I was devastated.

One scene was played over and over throughout our relationship.

She would promise to rub my back. "I'll do it later," she said, "with oil."

I eagerly awaited it, gazing from my chair at her body stretched out on the bed while she read. Looking at her made me want to touch her. I went over to the bed, reached under her sweater, rubbed my hands up and down the soft skin of her back. I leaned down further and kissed her cheek.

"I'm in love with Angela and Angela doesn't know what to do with me." I tried to keep my singsong voice playful. She squirmed uncomfortably at the teasing and made a great show of concentrated attention to her book. I returned to my chair.

The phone rang, and my stomach lurched at the interruption. I knew from her intimate tone that she was talking to a man. It was a tone I wished to hear directed at me. My stomach flurries became great waves of agitation.

When she hung up and returned to the bed, I went to her again, began touching her. Her stiffening body was the only acknowledgment of my caresses.

"Time for your back rub," she said after a few moments, snaking away from my hands. "Lie there. I'll get the oil."

When she came back I could feel her discomfort, but I didn't care. She was going to touch me. She raised my shirt, poured oil onto my back, began massaging it into my skin. And she talked. Irrelevancies. Problems with the children. Problems with Barry. I didn't care. She was touching me. She paused for a moment. I reached back and took hold of her hands. I felt her fear. She pulled away.

"It's uncomfortable for me," she said.

"Why?" I asked. "Because it's taboo?"

"I don't know. I'm just not comfortable with it. A hug or a kiss now and then, rubbing your back, that's okay."

"I'm in love with you," I said. "Do you love me?"

"Yes . . . very much, as a friend. I've never loved a woman as much as I love you, but I'm not in love with you."

I turned over onto my back, mouth dry with apprehension but unable to stop my words. "I want you to know how I feel. You're the most important person in my life. I want to be absolutely committed to you. I want to be your lover. I want to take care of you. I want to live with you. I want to give you everything."

"I can't love you like that now," she said.

"What does that mean?"

"Isn't it clear? I can't love you like that now or a month from now or maybe ever." She paused and, in the pause, abandoned equivocation. "You can *never* be my lover. I

(144)

only want heterosexual love. I simply don't feel for you the things I feel for a man."

"Then you'll have to help me," I said.

"How?" She was genuinely puzzled.

"Tell me to get lost, to leave you alone. It hurts so much, loving you, wanting you. I know you need a lot of people in your life, that I can't be all things to you, even if I'd like to be. But I could at least be *more* to you than I am now."

"You'll have to decide if it hurts too much and what you want to do about it. Maybe you'll choose to change our relationship."

I rose from the bed, crossed over to the refrigerator to get a beer. Turning back to her, I said: "I choose to love you."

I sat on the edge of the bed while we shared the beer. She talked warmly of the man on the phone. I listened, watching her intently in the half-dark, her milky skin luminous, dark eyes gleaming.

She emptied her glass, lay back on the bed, arms stretched upward, hands tucked under her head, curious eyes gazing straight at me.

I gave her a smile filled with love, then stretched toward her, my arms going round her neck, my lips brushing her cheek. She quickly turned away, rolling onto her side, back to me. I grabbed my pillow and curled myself around it, turning my back to her, feeling the warm tears run down my cheeks, spreading into a damp circle on the sheet.

In the fall of 1976 I was desolate. I knew my clinging to Angela was senseless and destructive, but I couldn't let go. I knew I was standing still, but I didn't know how to pull myself out of inertia. I'd had several unsatisfactory sexual encounters with men, devoid of any emotional content except fear that I'd do whatever they wanted, that I interested them only as a sexual outlet. I was increasingly suspicious of my father's conduct with my daughters, sickened by recollections of his past behavior with me. Relations with my partners in the new bookstore were deteriorating. I was hostile and unaccommodating to them. Then I happened on a brochure for a women writers' center in Connecticut, a school focused on feminist history and literature, run by feminists for feminists. I felt I'd been thrown a lifeline. My old desire to write and my new interest in feminism joined in a single enterprise—it must be a sign.

Immediately I filled out an application and sent along a covering letter that conveyed my desperation, not even certain what I had in mind but feeling instinctively that here was an out.

"I'm thirty-two years old," I wrote, "separated and about to be divorced. I have two small children and a great interest in writing. I want to write about women's issues. I have a story about incest. I'm unable to consider moving to Connecticut at this time. Please advise."

I heard within a week that I was welcome to attend a special session for one week in December, the courses to be taught by visiting, and eminent, authors. I sold my diamond engagement ring to raise tuition money, stripping away a piece of the past into the bargain. I'd devoted years of my life to securing this symbol of security. It was fitting, I thought, that it was the first thing to go when I determined to get out, get away.

I'd read one of Polly Grathwohl's novels before traveling to the center and I expected to like her. But when she strode into class that first morning I was truly dazzled. I fell in love on the spot. She was everything I wanted to be and was not: a successful writer with a splashy reputation, prominent in the women's movement, massively confident, clearly in charge of her life.

I watched her closely, inventorying every detail of her dress and manner: the shiny black hair that she habitually flipped back from her forehead with her right hand, the ring shaped like a star on her left hand, the ropes of gold looping onto the bulky sweater, the monogrammed pants cuff, the enchanting smile that lit up the room when it flashed across her mouth. Gazing at her, fascinated, I wondered what her body looked like beneath the clothes and still slightly shocked myself with this reflection.

I would gladly have handed my life over to her at that moment. As it turned out, it took a few days longer. I danced with her at a party that first night, amazed at how good it felt to hold her in my arms. The next day I tested her interest in me by leaving a group of women with whom we were drinking coffee in the cafeteria, returning to the classroom early, wondering if she'd follow me. She did. As she busied herself scribbling things on the blackboard, I stared at her wordlessly, relishing the current I felt flowing between us. The next evening I was invited to her house. Rushing through the cold darkness to get there, I felt certain she intended to act on this attachment I felt growing between us. When I arrived and found other people present, I was crushed, reduced again to adoring her from afar, feeling out of my depth in the conversation, trying to outstay the other guests, failing.

The next night, however, it finally happened, a ritual initiation not unlike another in my life so many years before. It was three o'clock in the morning, and I'd smoked marijuana for the first time. I floated alongside her as she led me up the stairs toward the bedroom.

Stopping before a doorway in the hall, she said, "This is the bathroom. There's a shower inside the tub. Here's a towel for you. If you're going to take a shower, don't flush the toilet first or you'll run out of water."

Did she want me to take a shower? Was this her way of suggesting one? I would have felt hopelessly awkward even with all my wits intact. The pot had completely obliterated any sharpness I might have had.

"I guess I'll take a shower," I finally stammered.

"You're going to have me dirty. I'm too tired to wash." She grinned and wafted off down the hall.

Inside the bathroom I stared into my own eyes in the mirror, terrified at what lay ahead. You are going to bed with that woman, I told my image, *that woman,* the teacher, the star. She knows a lot and you know nothing. Haven't you gotten yourself in a little too deep for comfort?

My answer was to get under the shower, standing beneath it until the water turned cold. Drying myself off slowly, postponing the moment as long as possible, I discovered my period had begun.

"What're you doing in there?" I heard her yell. "If you don't hurry up I'll fall asleep."

"Just a minute," I called out, trying to sound casual.

I brushed my teeth, looked in the cabinet over the sink for some deodorant. Despite the cool temperature, I was sweating from nervousness. Even the chilly floor of the hallway didn't cool me off as I padded toward her room.

Inside the door I stopped. She was curled up in some blankets on the far edge of the double mattresses that served as a bed, a single candle burning in a nearby corner.

"It must be fifty below in here," I murmured, still sweating even so, disconcerted by my nakedness.

(1 4 8)

"C'mon, before you freeze," she said, pulling aside the blankets to reveal her own body, inviting me in.

I quickly complied, her arms surrounding me as I lowered myself onto the bed, my breath disappearing as our bodies twined together.

"You have a beautiful body," she said.

"I take karate." It sounded ridiculous, but I had to say something. "It keeps me in shape."

"Well, don't ever stop," she said. "I like strong, muscular bodies."

She pulled me over on top of her, my body stretched along the length of hers. I was astonished by what I felt, great waves of emotion breaking over me, making me cry. She discovered this when her hands played over my face.

"What's the matter?" she asked.

I couldn't say: I've never been with a woman before. I couldn't say: so this is how it feels. I couldn't speak at all. I certainly couldn't act. But somehow she knew and took charge, leading me along with soft suggestions, gently guiding my hands where she wanted them to go.

Transported beyond my clumsiness and self-consciousness, I covered her face with kisses, murmured in her ear the thoughts I'd carried since that first day in class.

"You're so beautiful. You feel so good. I've wanted you every minute of this week."

"I'm just a *now*," she said, an edge in her voice that disturbed me even though I couldn't identify it.

It was, of course, a warning—but one I wouldn't have heeded even if I'd recognized it.

I returned home from the center filled with thoughts and fantasies of Polly but with no certain expectation of ever seeing her again. A few days later I received a letter from her detailing her speaking schedule for the next three months, including her address in London, where she intended to be over the approaching Christmas holidays. A few days after that she called to say the London trip had been canceled. Could she come and spend Christmas with me?

I was ecstatic. My feelings were reciprocated. *She* wanted to be with *me*. What I'd felt with her had been real. And I was scared. She'd see me in my own milieu and know how ordinary and confused I really was. She'd see an unexceptional bourgeois mother-housekeeper who could just barely cope. Nevertheless, I said yes. I was ready to relinquish my life again and nothing could have stopped me. I didn't recollect the cautionary note I'd heard in her voice the first night we spent together. I didn't stop to question why she wasn't spending the holidays with family or close friends. I just said yes, of course, come immediately, launching myself into my greatest exercise in unreality so far.

She stayed for two weeks, and each day was more filled with bliss, pleasure, satisfaction than the one before. Sexually, she was tender, sensitive, attuned to my needs, helping me to discover hers. She seemed to enjoy my children, watching them intently as they played, delighting in the time they spent with us. She automatically shared the household duties, washing dishes, cooking, shopping. I would never have thought to solicit her help. She was unfailingly patient and understanding as I talked about myself. When I said, "My life's such a mess," she didn't turn away. She held me closer and encouraged me to look for solutions.

Near the end of her stay, spellbound by her attentions,

growing accustomed to an intimacy I'd never enjoyed with anyone, I decided to tell her about my father and me. Trepidation made my mouth dry, my hands icy cold. The turbulence in my stomach pushed me close to nausea.

"Years ago I had sex with my father." I uttered it in a rush, almost unable to hear it because of the whooshing noise filling my ears.

She didn't recoil. She didn't even flinch. "That's happened to a lot of people," she said, almost nonchalantly.

"I've never told anyone before."

"I'm glad you could tell me."

Lightheaded with relief, eager to be rid of this old, old secret, I talked about it then for the first time. Putting my memories into words was excruciating and soothing at once. Dredging up a piece of that terrible history, saying it aloud, it felt more acute than ever. The moment I'd said it—and she was still listening, nodding understandingly—it seemed almost to evaporate. These dark pieces of myself, shielded from the air so rigorously for so long, appeared to disintegrate when they hit the light.

By the time Polly left she'd devised a plan for my life. In a month or so, during a break in her speaking tour, we'd go house-hunting near the writers' center, where she'd arranged for a teaching position, where I would begin work on a book about incest. We would buy the house together, equal shares, and live there with my children like a family. Now it was a toss-up as to which was greater: my love for her or my gratitude to her for telling me what to do with my life.

Portents existed even during these early days. She went through my house pointing out which items I should bring east, which I should leave behind. We didn't want any "tacky suburban furniture," she noted. We also would have no place for my dog, she told me—the ten-year-old schnauzer Roger had given me as a wedding gift, an animal I'd grown to love. The indications of this last dictate were too horrible to contemplate. So I didn't. Any and all alarm bells were muffled by my euphoria.

Emily, now six, and Julia, who was four, had grown rather accustomed to change. They'd seen their father leave and come back and leave again. They'd spent time with him in other places, living with him on weekends, returning to me for the week. They'd grown used to Angela being around, and then not. They'd watched Polly assume center stage in my life. And they liked her. She'd dazzled them by teaching them the latest dances, letting them wear her jewelry, telling them stories about life in other places. But nothing could have prepared them for the upheaval of moving across the country, leaving behind everyone and everything they'd ever known.

Even as the time for the move approached and I felt the overwhelming fear of venturing into the unknown, watched my children traumatized by the imminent separation from their father, saw the house I'd loved stripped bare, I never thought of pulling back. Even as I left my beloved dog alone in the empty house, knowing she'd be picked up the next day and put to sleep, knowing it because I'd arranged it, I didn't consider retreating. When I can bear to think of this—not often and not without unrelenting shame—it shows me how deeply I was caught again in the inexorable pattern: putting an authority in charge of my life, doing anything to gain approval, anything to avoid rejection, abdicating all my rights, willing to be used in return for love, clouding reality in fantastical mists. I was doomed, it seems, to play it out yet another time.

In a sense my relationship with Polly was over before it even began, similar in that way, too, to my marriage. Just as Roger stopped considering my needs as soon as he had me enthralled, so Polly's sensitivity and understanding vanished the moment my commitment was clear.

Arriving in Chesterton, Connecticut, the children and I waited two hours at the airport before one of Polly's hangers-on arrived to pick us up. Susanna would be "working" for us, Polly informed me, living in the house, helping us redecorate. She'd also take care of the children when I chauffeured Polly to speaking engagements.

Emily and Julia quickly responded to this arrangement with jealousy and resentment.

"All you care about is Polly." Emily began to throw this accusation at me every time I left the house.

Julia, in her fashion, clung to me ferociously, wordlessly, tears streaming down her face.

"I miss that house on the river," Emily would say wistfully, unmoved by the charms of the hundred-year-old Victorian Polly and I had purchased. "I miss Daddy and Gretel and Auntie Ellen and Grandpa and Grandma and the neighbors. . . ."

Julia, keenly attuned to my feeling for Polly and quite threatened by it, tried to come between us whenever she could, literally pushing her body between ours when we sat together, creating disturbances to interrupt our conversations.

The interest Polly had shown in the children now seemed nonexistent. She requested that they not share meals with us but be fed early. She competed with them for my attention.

"Who do you love more, them or me?" she'd ask.

"I can't choose between you," I answered. "I love you all differently, not one more than the other."

This was unacceptable. As her lover, she insisted, I should love her most.

"I don't cook," she announced soon after I arrived, "and I don't have time to do things around the house."

Uncomplaining, I assumed the burden of household chores and begged off the driving duties, which took me away from the children.

"You'd better think about what you're going to do for money," she told me. "This time you'll have to make it on your own."

Roger was withholding a large portion of my divorce settlement and money was indeed tight. I began working part time for a local real estate firm.

I was now in almost precisely the same position I'd been in during my marriage: running a house, working (both at real estate and on my book), suffering from emotional deprivation, quietly accumulating anger at the injustice of it all. I'd gleaned my previous identity from Roger and his family. Now my definition was as Polly's satellite. The level of communication between us was as superficial as that between Roger and me. The loneliness I felt was, very quickly, just as great. My sense of rejection, abandonment, was hauntingly familiar.

Running alongside the pain induced by my situation with Polly was the anguish I felt at unfolding the incest story. The only bright light came when I read a *People* magazine article about a man in California who counseled incest victims and offenders. Incest, he said, was not the victim's fault. What I'd always felt instinctively, my father's opinion to the contrary, had been confirmed by an expert. *I was not to blame.*

The comfort I took in this was enormous, but it was quickly swallowed up by my growing depression and desperation. When I forced Polly into a discussion about her withdrawal from me, I again heard echoes of the past.

"It's work that's important, Katherine, not love," she said. "I put all my emotions into work."

Just as Roger had seemed during our marriage to turn into my father, now Polly appeared to be turning into Roger.

"God, I'm sick of hearing about your past and present problems," she yelled at me one night. "And I'm tired of giving you answers for your life. Can't you do anything for yourself?"

I couldn't answer her.

"You'd do anything for approval. You feared rejection so much you fucked your father. You must have really been something! Look at you now. You're so dumb, so passive, so tuned out, I can't bear the sight of you. Anyone who fucks her father has to have something missing."

I retreated to my room in tears. This was what I'd feared most all those years. If I told about the incest it would somehow be used against me. Now it had happened. And it had the power to pulverize me. I felt, quite literally, as though I were crumbling.

This time I'd turned my life over to someone who didn't want it. Why had I done that? And why was I so passive, so unable to take possession of myself? Why did I always have the feeling that my life was over there when I was standing here? Why did everything seem to be repeating itself?

I didn't fully recognize then all the connections to my

incestuous past. But I did sense that I mustn't keep any part of it buried any longer. No matter how painful, I would have to explore it fully and get help with whatever feelings my explorations produced.

So when Andy visited me in Chesterton in May, I gave him a draft of my manuscript to read. He reacted with numbing shock, terrible anger toward Dad, and a growing sense of mission to return home and warn Mother of what lay ahead, tell Dad what he thought of him. It was not a mission he ever carried out, nor would I have wished him to. It was time for me to face my parents myself.

CHAPTER

12

"*I'm sorry I have caused you so much trouble. I guess I thought love was the answer to all our problems.*"

—*Dad*

"*As a mother I probably fell very short of what you children think I should have done. Maybe I am innocent and naive, but I did the best I knew how.*"

—*Mother*

I was thirty-three years old in the summer of 1977. I looked more like forty-five. The emotional strain of the months just past and of what lay ahead had left me pallid and spent. Great dark patches formed half-moons beneath my eyes. My skin had a slightly gray tinge. New lines cut into my cheeks and drew my mouth downward.

As I flew toward Great Rapids in August, two strains of thought struggled with each other: optimism and apprehension. Maybe exposure would, ultimately, allow us to be the normal happy family we'd never been. Maybe it would cause the whole family to turn against me. The latter strain was decidedly stronger.

The first few hours in my family's house I basked in the sense of familiarity, comforting after my exile in alien territory. It was soothing to be someplace where it was appropriate for me to be a child. I didn't have to think of my difficulty selling real estate, sustaining relationships, coping with my own children. Here they were the adults; I was the child. I didn't have to perform as a grown-up.

We sat in the kitchen, Mother and I at the table, Dad off to the side in his rocker. The talk was superficial; coin of the realm in this household. Mother, an expert on anything she'd seen covered for five minutes on the *Today* show, did most of it.

"I am just amazed," she hummed on, "at the things people talk about today, things that used to be absolutely taboo. Why, on television the other day I even heard a report about incest."

What an opening! Now was my chance. As I tried to summon enough air to push out the words, my father leaped in to steer us onto another subject. I can't tell them together, I thought. I never could talk to them at the same time. Why should it be any different now?

"I'm going to take a walk, get some air," I said. What I really wanted was a cigarette and a chance to think. Smoking had become a compulsion with me, but one I'd never exhibited in front of my parents. With them, their child once again, I hadn't the right to smoke.

"Want some company?" Dad asked.

"Sure. Why not?" He didn't hear my reticence. Now I couldn't have the cigarette. Now I'd also have to try to talk to him.

"Let's go up toward the hospital," he suggested as we headed down the front walk, reaching an arm around my waist to turn me in the right direction, setting a swift pace.

We moved along in a silence broken only by an occasional reminiscent note from me when a house, a tree, a particular street ignited my memory. In my mind I was auditioning lines to open a real conversation. It seemed I tried dozens. The longer I waited, the harder it would be to begin. Finally I just blurted out the simplest, most direct beginning I could think of.

"Let's talk about us, Dad," I said, feeling his body tighten immediately with wariness. "It's important for me to tell you how I feel and what it's done to me. I've tried before, but I don't think you understood me."

"You know I always loved you and never took advantage of you," he said, getting his rationalization on record at the outset.

"But that's just it, Dad. You did take advantage of me. I was a child."

"But I never forced you," he protested, shoving aside my contention, harking back to his perpetual point of honor.

"You did, Dad, not with violence but in subtle, manipulative ways."

"And there were plenty of times I could've," he went on, as though I hadn't spoken. "Do you remember the time you and your ma got so drunk and I had to take you both home and undress you and put you to bed?"

"That was the night we celebrated my engagement to Roger."

"Well, you really got me excited that night." The recollection made his voice husky. He reached out to take hold of my arm. "I put Ma to bed first and then I came into your room and undressed you. My God, you had a gorgeous figure and I got a bad hard-on. It wasn't easy for me not to crawl into bed with you. Your ma was out cold. She would never have known."

I was trying hard to stay calm. I needed us to understand

each other. "But, Dad," I reminded him, "I wouldn't have let you get into bed with me that night. Don't you remember that I said no to you?"

"I still could have forced you, and I didn't."

We were miles apart. I wanted him to assume more responsibility; he wanted credit for his restraint.

"I brought along an article that I want you to read," I said. "It's written by the director of a child sexual abuse center in California where they deal with incest like ours. There was also a three-hour television special about the center recently. I wish you could have seen it."

"I think your ma saw part of it," he grumbled.

"The fathers took full responsibility for what happened between them and their daughters."

"I still think you were responsible too," he said, the old petulance sounding in his words.

"I know you do. And it's true that I acquired some sexual skills through you and that I also came to manipulate and use you. But I wasn't responsible for the beginning. *I was only a child.*"

My repetition of this phrase, my heavy accent on each word, left him speechless for a moment. He seemed to think about what I'd said, not even bothering to trot out his line about what a little tease I was. He just stared straight ahead, striding along beside me silently.

"Sometime I'd like to go to the center and receive counseling," I said. "Would you mind if I did?"

"I never knew you thought you needed help with that." He was genuinely surprised.

"I know you didn't. I could never make you understand how I felt. And I could never tell anyone else. But I realize now that it disturbs me terribly and I have to find some way to get over it. Have you ever talked to anyone about it?"

"No, but you know I had to take twelve hours of psychology courses for my job."

I refrained from leaping on the irrelevance of that statement and continued with my train of thought. "Would you talk to anyone about it now?" I asked. "Would you go with me to talk to someone?"

"I don't think so," he said casually. "I just don't feel a need to. I think if two people are attracted to each other it's okay for them to have sex. The sexual revolution has done that for us."

"Even when it's your own daughter?"

"Sure, why not? It seems natural."

His inclusion of incest in a list of the by-products of sexual liberation shocked me. He seemed able to turn anything to his advantage. I hid my dismay, however, and decided to try another tack.

"You must have been going through a real bad time in your life when we began, weren't you, Dad?" I was still trying to give him the benefit of the doubt, to offer him avenues of redemption.

"Well, sure. You know how your ma is about sex. I just wasn't getting what I needed." He continued to refuse any and all openings. "Some people just need more sex than others. I've told you that before."

"I don't care what you needed, Dad. It wasn't right for you to use me."

"I can't have sex unless it's someone I'm really attracted to, like you. I couldn't use a prostitute because of my job. I told you that before." This was to him a sensible rationale. It baffled him that I couldn't understand the simple logic of it. "Some call it chemistry, I don't know. I just know I had that feeling for you. I still do. I could still go to bed with you and feel good about it."

His sidelong glance and fatuous giggle made my skin prickle unpleasantly.

"Of course, you don't want to, do you?" he continued, unable to disguise the note of hope in his voice.

"That's right, Dad. I don't want to." I tried to hide my revulsion. If I let it surface, I wouldn't be able to go on talking to him. "You're my father and I care about you as a daughter. It's concern I feel, not sexual desire."

I was talking to him now as though he were a child, and he responded like a defensive little boy.

"Well," he blustered, "I just did what I thought was right. As far as I'm concerned, I taught you everything you needed to know."

I cut him off, unwilling to hear this argument one more time. "Would you mind if I talked to that man in California?" I asked.

He hesitated a beat before answering. "No, I guess not. But I just hope you won't use it against me. I'd do anything for you, Kathy. You know that, don't you?"

A score of sarcastic replies flew into my head. Immediately, my censorship mechanism, the cornerstone of my docility, erased them. I still needed to hear the loving words, no matter how his performance belied them.

"I don't know," I murmured, "I only know that back then I started to get into real trouble in my head. I felt guilty, ashamed. I couldn't confide in anyone. Do you have any idea how depressed it made me?"

"Sure, I knew you felt bad. But I thought it was because you weren't getting enough sex."

"No, Dad." I was weary now, as though I'd been slog-
ging through a muddy field, sinking in to my knees with
every step, tugging against a downward pull each time I
hauled one foot out to put it in front of the other. "I was
depressed because I didn't know what to do about it. Do
you think Mother knew what was going on?"

"No, never." He waved away the possibility with his
hand. "She's naive. She believes in people. She doesn't like
to think about the bad things that could happen between
them."

Here was his admission that he *did* recognize what we'd
done was wrong, an admission I'd wished, pleaded, and
prayed for. I didn't even bother to seize on it, knowing it
would just lead him back to his timeworn rationalizations:
*never took advantage . . . taught you what I knew . . . who'd
we hurt . . . little tease.*

"Do you know the only way I could figure out to help
myself?" I asked.

"What?"

"Marrying Roger. I knew I had to get away from you,
but I wasn't strong enough to do it alone. I thought he'd
protect me and take care of me, so I married him."

"I thought that was a mistake, you know," he said, sail-
ing past the substance of what I'd said. "I really wanted to
see you out in the world. You belong out there. Remember
I told you I'd send you to college?"

"I didn't want to be obligated to you financially. If I
were, I thought, I'd have to take care of you sexually again,
and I couldn't face that. Anyway, I was afraid to go out
into the world. I was afraid to grow up."

"It did seem strange," he mused, "a good-looking girl
like you still living at home at twenty-one."

"Of course it did," I concurred. "I was all messed up ... and I still am."

"What do you mean?" He was shocked, as though he'd heard nothing of the preceding conversation. "You seem okay to me."

"Dad,"—I pushed the word through gritted teeth— "I can't get along with other people. I don't trust anyone ... or I trust them too much. I have a regular pattern of destroying relationships. I'm hopelessly dependent. ...." I ran out of steam and broke off listing my liabilities.

"You're just having trouble because of this divorce thing you're going through."

"That's part of it," I conceded, "but so is the incest. I can't straighten out anything until I take care of that. I have two children to raise and at the moment I'm in no shape to do it. I need to get help."

"Do whatever you think you have to do."

We finished our walk in silence, bodies synchronized, minds asunder. Just the way it had always been.

The next day I watched for an opportunity to talk to my mother alone. Dad must have known what I had in mind and, trying to postpone the inevitable, didn't let her out of his sight until mid-afternoon, when she went into the backyard to pull weeds from her flower garden. I settled down near where she was working, sunning myself. Eventually, giving her back a rest, she turned to talk to me.

"Your father's awful antsy," she said. "What's wrong with him?"

"How's he treating you?" I asked, avoiding her question.

"He's not good ... moody, pouting, same old thing. His nose is out of joint because Grandma's here."

"Same old story. He never could stand her to visit. He told me last night he hates to see you dote on her."

"She's eighty-four years old," Mother protested, "and she's been very sick."

"You don't have to justify it to me," I assured her. "I think you should take care of her."

"Part of his problem is that he hasn't got enough to do. He gardens a little, gabs with the fellows he runs into at the supermarket, but not much else. He won't go out and take a course at the college for next to nothing. He refuses to do volunteer work. He doesn't need a job because of his pension."

"What about you? What do you do?"

"I keep busy, go about my business, do whatever I like. And that's okay with him."

Once again, I knew I had to take the plunge, knew I wouldn't if I waited for the perfect opening.

"Mother, he's got a life of his own too, you know."

"What do you mean?" She smiled at me, eyes squinting against the sun.

"I want to tell you something about Dad and me . . . for my sake and for both of yours as well." I could feel my eyes filling, my throat closing, as I spoke. "I hope you're strong enough to hear what I have to say."

A troubled look replaced her smile, and she grew very still.

"Dad and I had an incestuous relationship."

I fixed my eyes intently on her face, searching for any flicker of knowledge, any trace of recognition. She didn't wince; she didn't look shocked.

"Oh, no, honey." Her voice was soft as she gazed back at me. Then she dropped her eyes. "Well," she said, even more quietly, "I wondered."

She knew, I thought. She'd always known. Anger at her betrayal made my whole body start to shake.

(1 6 5)

"It started when I was eight in Hartland and I'd crawl into bed with him." I could see my words stinging her, and I was glad they hurt. "At first he just fondled me, but eventually he did other things. And to this day he thinks what he did was right. He thinks because he loved me he had a right to me sexually."

"Oh, God, Kathy, how awful for you." Her anguish was genuine, but at that moment I didn't care.

"For years I couldn't tell anyone about it. I wanted to tell you but I was sure you'd think it was my fault. I thought you wouldn't love me anymore, and I couldn't risk that. I needed your love and I needed his. God knows, I wouldn't have been in the situation in the first place if I hadn't been so desperate for his love."

"Oh, I'm so sorry, honey. I'm so sorry you had to endure all that."

"Mother, did you ever know about it?"

"No, never." Her eyes flew up to my face with her quick reply. "Well, it may have flashed through my mind a couple of times, but nobody talked about incest back then. Kathy, you should have told me."

I wanted to say: *Mother, you should have asked.* Instead I asked her what she would have done if I had told her.

"I'd have divorced him. I almost did anyway. He was impossible to live with sometimes."

"I guess unconsciously I felt you wouldn't do anything about it. I felt you'd take his side."

"I would have divorced him," she repeated. "Oh, honey . . ." Her voice trailed off as she slid back into the past.

"Were you jealous of me?" I asked.

She stared toward her flower bed, eyes clouded by reflection. "No . . . not jealous. I used to wonder, though, why he always insisted you come out to dinner with us. It didn't make sense to me. But no, I wasn't jealous. I was hurt that he made your life so miserable, setting down such tight restrictions, calling the police, watching every move you made."

"He told me you never gave him enough sex. He said that's why he had to turn to me."

"That is a lie," she cried, her voice made shrill by outrage. "I never said no to him, even when my back was so bad and I was in pain. Never!"

"Lying bastard," I muttered. "What a double standard he lives by . . . and the governor gave him an award for thirty years of enforcing the law."

"Have you told your brother?"

"Yes. He's very angry with Dad and very concerned about you."

"Ellen? Have you told her?"

"I've hinted at it."

"Don't tell her, Kathy. I don't think she could handle it."

"I think she can, Mother. And now's a good time, while she's seeing a psychiatrist."

"I didn't know that. She should have told me."

"Mother, try to face it. This is a family of secrets. We don't even really know each other because none of us can be honest about what we feel. We go along, propped up by our happy-family facade, but none of the real problems get solved. Ellen should have seen a doctor years ago, when her school counselor advised it. Andy's twenty-nine and he hasn't the slightest notion of what to do with his life. It's clear the kind of shape I'm in due to prolonged avoidance of reality, and now you're stuck dealing with a problem that's more than twenty years old. We're a mess, Mother. I'd say the facade is wearing pretty thin."

It was, in fact, about to tear wide open. The atmosphere in the house was crackling with tension, humming with unspoken undercurrents. Mother was hurt, resentful, and uncertain what to do with her feelings, confused about possible courses of action. Dad, despite his ignorance of my talk with Mother, was extremely edgy, wary of both of us. I was wretched, disturbed by my divorce-settlement dispute with Roger as well as by the situation with my parents, finding it difficult to eat or sleep, physically and emotionally exhausted.

I tried to enlist Ellen's support when we met one day for lunch. In typical family fashion, she preferred to look the other way.

"It's just all so sick," she said, aversion evident in the set of her mouth. "What are you going to do?"

"I'm going to California to talk to Doug Giancani, and I hope I can get both Mom and Dad to come with me."

"It all happened so long ago," she said. "Why not just forget it?"

I told her I couldn't do that, but I don't think she understood.

Later that day I outlined Mother's alternatives for her.

"You have some choices," I told her. "You can ask him to leave. You can say you've had enough of his terrible behavior and demand that he get some help, offering to go with him if he likes. You can tell him I've told you about the incest and offer to discuss it with him. Or I can sit down with the two of you and tell you how I feel and ask you both to come to California with me."

"Oh, I couldn't go, Kathy," she said.

You coward! You still can't face reality. As quickly as the thought flashed across my mind, I squelched it. Her refusal, I believed, carried a clear message: this thing is your problem and you'd better solve it. Taken one step further, the message read: this thing was your fault in the first place. Just what I'd always feared she would think. I couldn't stand it. I buried it all.

"I've got to take Grandma back home and stay with her awhile. Everyone else is away."

"Couldn't Ellen take her?"

"No . . . I just don't think she's up to that."

A scream formed in my mind: What about me? What about what I'm up to? I didn't utter it.

"I don't know what to do about your father," she went on. "I'm afraid of what he might do. What if he tries to kill himself . . . or one of us?"

I just laughed, not kindly but with derision. "You know, I used to be afraid of Roger, afraid he'd become violent if I stood up to him. But do you know what happened when I finally did? He cried like a little boy whose mother wouldn't give him his way."

"He has a gun, you know."

"If you'll sleep better, we can hide it. And if you like, I'll ask him to go to California with me. He said he'd do anything for me. Let's see if he means it."

"Oh, yes, why don't you do that? Then maybe he and I can talk about it when he gets back."

Her gratitude for this remedy was pathetic. She was so relieved to be off the hook. You handle him, Kathy; I just don't know what to do. Here we go again.

I asked my father that night to help me with the dishes.

"Okay, Sport," he quickly agreed.

"What's the matter?" I asked him when we were alone in the kitchen. "You seem upset."

"It's Grandma," he said snappishly. "No matter what I do, I get her stuck down my throat. I worked thirty years to own this house and here I am sleeping in the basement so she can be in my bed."

"You agreed to let her come to visit, didn't you?"

"It wouldn't have mattered if I did or not." He grew more irritated as he thought about his grievances. "Your ma always takes care of her family first and to hell with me. I just want to be here alone with Mother. I don't like people living with us, and if I were sixty-five I'd sell this damn place and get out of here once and for all."

"I know it's been hard for you to have me here with all my problems," I said.

"No, not at all," he answered. "But your ma should have gone to that baseball game with me today and instead I had to go alone."

"Is Grandma the only reason you're so hard to live with?"

"I don't know." He was reluctant to continue but finally did. "I guess I just feel out of place. You guys don't need me. I'm just in the way."

"Do you feel that with Mother? Is that why you can't get along?"

"I don't feel it when it's just her and me."

"She tells me you're horrible; you tell me she's horrible. Maybe you two ought to split up for a while."

"No, we don't need to do that." He was surprised by my suggestion and rejected it firmly. "We just need to be alone."

"Dad, I'm going to that counseling place in California. Why don't you come along?"

"Oh, I couldn't do that." He echoed my mother almost exactly. "No, that would be too hard for me."

"You said you'd do anything for me. Will you do this?"

The apprehension he felt at the prospect made the plate he was drying quiver in his hands. He set it back in the rack. "And what if I'm the monster you say I am?" he said. "What will happen to me?"

"You'll understand yourself better. That's all that will happen. Besides," I added, "you'll be helping me."

"What will Mother and Grandma think?"

"They'll think you're on a business trip with me."

"You mean we should lie to them?" He obviously found this thought immoral, however expedient.

"They don't have to know everything. When you get back you can tell Mother whatever you like. I think she knows something's up anyway. I think she's always known."

"I'll have to think about it," he said, just as my mother and grandmother wandered in from the back porch.

"I'm going to California on a business trip," I announced, "and I want Dad to go with me but he doesn't want to."

"Why not?" Mother asked him.

"We can't afford it," he grumbled.

"Sure we can, Tom," she said. "We've got enough money. Go along with her."

"I don't know," he answered. "I'll have to think about it."

When the day of my departure arrived, he still hadn't declared his intentions.

"Your father's gone walking," Mother said, waking me early. "Do you think I should make a reservation for him?"

"Yes, go ahead," I said groggily. "I think he'll go."

Returning from his walk, he found Mother had a suitcase open on the bed, some clothes stacked neatly beside it.

"What's the idea?" he asked, knowing very well.

"You are going, aren't you?" It wasn't even really a question.

"Do you think I should?" he asked her.

"Yes, I do," she replied. "I think it'll do you good."

CHAPTER

13

*"I can imagine the session you had was bad.
What utter unhappiness in this world."*

—*Mother*

Before we even got on the plane I felt stifled by my father's presence. He was nervous, fidgety. I was inundated by memories. But already there had been a reversal of roles between us. I was the adult, he the child. This was my show; I was directing it.

"I feel like I'm being persecuted," he whined, the helpless victim.

"You're not," I replied, the firm, stern authority.

Our discomfort with each other grew during the long journey: an unexpected wait at the Great Rapids airport, a layover in Chicago, four more hours from there to Berkeley. When we arrived I made a pointed proposal.

"I'll call a hotel and get two single rooms," I said.

"Aw, let's get a double." He grinned broadly at me.

"I need my privacy," I said resolutely, trying to keep the internal quavers from showing.

"But rooms are so expensive," he argued. "If we share one, it'll be much cheaper."

"I'd still rather have my privacy," I repeated.

"Look," he said, "I know you're afraid to sleep in a room with me. But don't worry. I won't try anything."

I acquiesced, for financial reasons and because I thought if we stayed together we might be able to talk. As it was, we filled our first twenty-four hours in California with empty chatter. We'd arrived on a Saturday and weren't due to see Doug Giancani until Monday. We spent Sunday sightseeing, driving U.S. Highway 1 to San Francisco, visiting Fisherman's Wharf and Chinatown, crossing back and forth over the Golden Gate Bridge, babbling about smog, earthquakes, forest fires. He said often how much he missed Mother; he wondered what she was doing; he felt like half a person without her. We were both thinking of the next day. His apprehension, I was glad to see, was even greater than mine. I could almost feel him counting the minutes, and I enjoyed watching him sweat it out.

That night, back in the room, we did finally talk about the reason we were there. He wanted to hear a list of my complaints against him once more before we saw Doug the next day.

"I'm just so afraid I'm going to be a monster," he said when I'd finished, to me a tacit admission that he knew he had been one.

I also recalled how he'd treated Ellen, locking her out of the house, refusing her help in the early troubled years of her marriage.

"Was I really that hard?" he asked, not remembering, not wanting to.

"You were absolutely unbending," I told him, "unnecessarily harsh."

The next day we endured more waiting, having the morning to get through before our appointment, the anxiety almost unbearable now, Dad's still worse than mine. Waiting in Doug's office, Dad couldn't remain still. He'd sit for a minute or so, rise and pace up and down the room, flop back down into the chair, rise again. I tried to ignore him, diverting myself with the literature that was available.

In pamphlets published by the center I read about something called incest dread, a feeling that made accurate statistics hard to come by, a feeling that kept people from reporting cases of incest. It was known, however, that one of four girls in this country, before reaching eighteen, suffers sexual abuse. Seventy-five percent of the time, she knows her abuser; thirty-four percent of the time it's a member of her own household.

Doug entered, his relaxed presence and comforting voice helping immediately to still my qualms.

"I want to congratulate you both for coming," he said. "I can help you, but you should also know that you've already helped yourselves a great deal by making this trip together."

I felt this was a friend. It had taken me twenty-five years to find him, but finally I had someone on my side.

"I know you two have talked about the past," he said to my father. "Tell me how you feel about it, Thomas."

"Oh, well . . ." Dad broke off and squirmed uneasily in his chair. I liked seeing his distress, even as I reproved myself for enjoying it.

"Well," he began again, "I feel okay, I guess. I told Kathy I'd come here for her. I'm not afraid to do hard things. I've had to do hard things all my life."

Now he'd regained his composure and was blustering

along in his usual vein. "As far as this thing goes, I don't feel I did anything wrong. I just figured I was helping her, showing her what she needed to know so she wouldn't get in trouble like her sister did."

"Tell me about your past, Thomas," Doug said. "What plans did you have for your life?"

"During the war I left a good job in Chicago to join the Marines. I felt it was my duty to serve my country. My family's aggressive and they believe in fighting. My wife's family doesn't, so they condemned me and she never forgave me for joining up and leaving her when she was pregnant with Kathy. I didn't see Kathy until she was two years old."

He stopped, gazing in my direction with blind eyes, seeing his two-year-old baby daughter, not the adult child who was his accuser.

"I was taught discipline in the Marines," he continued, "and my job when I came back home was as a disciplinarian, a prison guard. But I guess I went too far with that. Kathy tells me I was too strict at home."

"What were your goals then, Thomas, when the war was over?"

"I wanted security, solid benefits, a good pension when I retired, so I took a job with the state."

"Do you feel you set high goals for yourself?" Doug asked.

"Yes, sir."

"Did you also set high moral standards?"

"That's right."

"Often when we do that, Thomas, when we're so strict with ourselves, something gives. Something gave with you. Do you know what it was?"

"No . . . not really," Dad stammered. "I don't really. I guess I turned into a monster."

"You're not a monster." Doug's voice was gentle, reassuring. "You're a human being. You've only been human."

Doug turned then to me and asked how I felt about coming to see him.

"Good," I answered quickly, "and necessary. I know it will help me, and I hope it helps my parents. They've been married almost forty years and they're just not getting along. They're at each other's throats all the time. I think if we deal with the incest it might clear the air for all of us."

"I agree," Doug said. "Tell me what positive things you see in your parents' marriage."

"I think they really love each other. I think, even in spite of the incest, they want to stay together."

"It sounds like a strong marriage, and that's a rare thing, very positive. What about you? How can all this be positive for you?"

"I'm not sure," I said. "I don't know."

"I do," he said quietly. "You're sensitive, compassionate, intuitive, and the incest has made you strong. You've had to be strong to survive. Let's go back to when it started. What do you remember, Kathy?"

When Doug suggested this journey to the past, I felt my eyes cloud over, my throat constrict. There was no more hiding now. I had to travel into the labyrinth, recall it all, record it aloud. Poised at the edge of the maze, I was terrified and exhilarated at once.

"I was about eight," I began. "Mother was away at night, working. The wind used to blow through the old boards of our house and make scary sounds, bang the shutters, whistle around the corners. And one night there was a storm and

I became frightened and went downstairs and crawled into bed with Dad. He began fondling me and I didn't know what to do."

The old sense of powerlessness flooded over me. I felt myself beginning to cry. "I didn't know what to do," I repeated.

"How did you feel?" Doug asked.

"I felt comforted, secure, safe. But I didn't like his voice. It was strange, creepy. And I didn't like it when he began comparing me to Mother."

"What do you remember about the beginning, Thomas?"

"We were always real affectionate with our kids; we'd hold them a lot. I'd sit in a chair and rock Andrew, Kathy's brother, and she'd always be right there wanting me to rock her too. So I'd put them both on my lap."

"What happened when you rocked Kathy?"

"I'd get excited."

"Do you mean you'd become aroused, get an erection?"

"Yes."

"What did you think about that?" Doug asked. "That it was bad or that it felt good?"

"That it felt good."

"Kathy, do you remember your father getting an erection?"

I nodded silently.

"What did you think about it?"

"I was curious and it interested me. Then Mother took me aside and told me not to sit on his lap anymore."

"I never knew about that," my father interrupted, obviously surprised.

"In fact, she told me not to sit on any man's lap."

"Did your mother tell you about sex?"

"Only in a very sketchy way. Nobody talked much about sex in those days, and the fact that she was a German Methodist didn't help."

"Sometimes," Doug said, "religions give us the idea that sex is bad. And it's not, of course. It's not bad to have sexual feelings. It's natural. I don't think our creator would have given us a sexual apparatus and function and then made the use of them bad. Thomas, what would you have thought if Kathy had sat on your brother's lap and your brother had had an erection and fondled her?"

"I would have hated it. I'd have killed him."

"Do you remember fondling Kathy?"

"Yes . . . but that's all I did when she crawled in bed with me. I only fondled her. I thought it was good for her, but I guess I was wrong. I shouldn't have done it."

"What did you say?" Doug asked quietly.

"I was wrong . . . I shouldn't have done it."

Hearing his words, I felt something in me yield This was what I'd wanted from him. Now he'd given it to me.

Doug's questions continued. "What was going on with you at that time, Thomas? With your job? With your wife?"

"My wife and I both worked because we needed the money. We didn't believe in baby-sitters. We thought a parent should be with the kids, so we arranged to work different hours. When I came home, she'd leave for work."

"So you didn't spend much time together?"

"That's right. My wife worked hard. Even when she was home she was usually tired."

"Did you feel you had enough sex with her?"

"I guess not. As I say, she was often tired."

"Could you talk to your wife about what you needed?"

"Not really."

"Could you talk to her if you had a problem at work?"

"No, I guess not. If I did that I'd feel sort of weak . . . you know. I tried not to bring my problems home. I tried to leave them at work."

"Could you cry in front of your wife?"

"No."

"How did Kathy help you?"

"She was always right there." My father's voice, which had been rather monotonous, now became warm, animated by his remembrance of me as a young girl. "She was my favorite child . . . still is . . . and we were real close. We did everything together: hunting, fishing, camping. You should have seen how she could pitch a tent. I was so proud of her."

"She brought you pleasure, didn't she? She brought you joy. And how was she different from your wife?"

"Well . . . in every way. She had . . . what is it they say? All the accessories."

"You mean she developed early?"

"Yes."

"And how was that different from your wife?"

"Well . . . she was flat-chested and Kathy was extremely the opposite."

"I know that really attracted him," I put in. "When he fondled me he often talked about my breasts and how they were so much bigger than Mother's."

"And she smelled good, didn't she, Thomas?" Doug went on.

Reverie made my father's voice foggy. "Oh, she was soft and affectionate and sweet, and her personality . . . it was just great."

"And she smelled good, right?"

"Yes, she smelled good too."

"Let me tell you about tenderness," Doug said to my father. "When Kathy sat on your lap, when she crawled into bed with you, she was seeking tenderness, which you needed at that time also but couldn't ask for from your wife."

Dad stared intently at Doug, following his thought, nodding.

"Your daughter gave you tenderness willingly, with love and trust. And when she did, you became aroused. This isn't unusual. It happens a lot. Mothers become aroused nursing their babies. A man came to me recently who had an erection while hugging his little boy. And he was appalled. He asked what was happening, what kind of person he was turning into. I told him what I'm telling you: it's natural and good. What is not natural and good is what people do after they become aroused. What you did with Kathy was not natural and good. You owe your daughter an apology, Thomas."

"Yes, sir," Dad said softly. "I know that now."

"You see," Doug emphasized, "you were the parent, she was the child. You were in control."

Dad gave another nod of acquiescence.

"How do you feel about each other now?" Doug asked. "Thomas, look at your daughter and tell her."

Dad turned to face me. "I love you just as much as I always have," he said. "I'm sorry I got you into this mess."

"Kathy," Doug prompted, "how do you feel?"

"Numb," I said, "and relieved . . . and I'm not angry anymore. I love my parents and I know they care for me. For years, in one way or another, I thought, This can't be happening to me. I'm glad I've finally faced the fact that it did."

My father agreed. "I also want to talk to my wife about all of this," he added, "and to my two other children."

At the end of our session Doug said he didn't think we needed further counseling, but cautioned that we'd both have work to do on our own. He suggested we stay until Wednesday to attend a meeting of Parents United, a group composed of the mothers and fathers of families in which incest has occurred.

Driving back to Berkeley, I felt buoyant. I had shed my twenty-five-year-old burden. My corrosive anger had vanished. Dad had said he loved me, that he'd been wrong, that he was sorry. This terrible ancient wound of mine had been ripped open and healed over in the course of a few short hours.

When we stopped along the way for a cold beer, I asked Dad if he'd stay for the meeting.

"I've been to that kind of thing, you know," he said. "I had to do it for my work. I know what it'll be like."

"I'm not sure you do," I pointed out. "You've never attended a meeting about incest."

Veering away from that subject, he asked if the session with Doug had satisfied me. I said it had and asked how he'd felt about it.

"Well, I'm not sure about his slant on this thing," he said. "I never thought we were hurting anyone. I thought it would be good for you."

I felt the rage begin to churn again in my stomach, to burn behind my eyes. I blotted out the rest of what he said as he sat drinking his beer, chanting the old litany, reverting to the old rationalizations, telling himself what he needed to hear to be able to go on living with himself.

Back at the motel, he began grumbling again about our

expensive room. He'd found a cheaper place on his morning walk and suggested we move there. We did, I following his directions like an automaton, trying to recall my earlier optimism, barely able to remember, let alone recapture, it. When we'd settled into the new double room, he set off on another of his walks, returning shortly before dinnertime.

"I don't see any real reason for me to stay," he said then. "Do you? I'll leave it up to you. If you want me to, I will."

I was too angry to speak coherently, angry that he wanted to leave, angry that he'd obliterated the positive aspects of the afternoon, angry that he was pushing responsibility onto me once again, asking me to decide if he should stay or go.

"I don't care what you do; do whatever you like" was the most I could manage.

He asked me to call the airport and make him a reservation for the following morning. Ever accommodating, I complied.

Our conversation that evening was perfunctory and cut mercifully short by going to bed early, both of us eager for the day to end. He awakened me the next morning at five-thirty, bringing me coffee and the news that he'd switched me into a single room, which would be cheaper still.

It was drizzly and gray outside, unusual for California in mid-August, and my mood matched the landscape. I felt very close to tears during the ride to the airport and the half-hour wait for his plane, but determined not to cry in front of him.

When his flight was announced, he slid quickly out of

the booth where we were drinking coffee, leaned over to hug me, and kissed me on the cheek.

"I'm sorry I got you into this." He repeated his line of the previous day. "I hope you can get out of it."

I watched his figure, blurred now by my brimming eyes, moving to get in line. Twice he turned to look back and wave at me. I stared in his direction, numb, hands in my lap, tears streaming down my cheeks. Finally I moved to the window, fixing my gaze on his plane, following it down the runway to takeoff, watching it disappear into the somber sky. Even after it vanished I stood unmoving, pinned in place by my feelings: anger, hurt, loneliness, and god-awful fear.

I got through that dismal day by the skin of my teeth, the sense of being alone almost unbearable, the fear nearly overwhelming. I couldn't eat, though I knew I should. I couldn't read. I wanted to make notes about the counseling session the day before, but it was difficult to remember clearly.

Early in the afternoon I fell asleep for a couple of hours, unusual for me, and when I awakened I called Polly. I wanted to tell her my plans. I wanted to hear a familiar voice.

"I'll probably be back in about a week," I told her. "I have a couple of business matters to see to in Great Rapids and I have to pick up the kids. Then I'll be back."

"Yes." The distance in her voice was more than geographical.

"I feel better now, better than I did when I left."

"I think you were right back in June," she said, ignoring my progress report. "You said then that we should live apart."

"I still want to be with you," I said. "Please let's try it again."

"No," she said offhandedly. "I've had a lot of time to think, and you were right. You should live alone for a while. Besides, you crowd me."

"But I'm healthier now . . . better."

"You have a long way to go," she said. "You won't be good for anyone for at least two years."

I didn't ask where in the world she got that figure. I was devastated, my feelings of desertion exacerbated by her indifference, my loneliness sharper than it had been before I'd called her.

Information gave me the phone number for the Berkeley University Women's Center, and I called there to ask where I could meet people. I felt I couldn't be alone. They had no concrete suggestions for me. I decided to walk the three miles to downtown Berkeley.

I know, difficult as it is even now for me to admit it, that what I had in mind was a sexual connection. My real need was for companionship, affection, reassurance. But I knew how to assuage that need only through a sexual channel.

I set out for downtown. I'd gone several blocks when a car pulled up to the curb, honking, two dubious-looking young men waving to me from the windows, inviting me in. I kept walking, but the paranoia had begun. I decided it wasn't safe on the streets and soon turned around and returned to my room.

I made myself eat although it was hard to swallow. I still couldn't read. I couldn't even watch television. I began to think of my father. Earlier that day, watching him board his plane, he'd seemed like a snake, slithering away, getting off easy. Now I wished he were here. I picked up the phone and called his number.

"Hi, Kathy," he said, sounding lighthearted, carefree.

"How was your trip?" I asked.

"Good . . . real smooth. It seemed faster coming back than it did going."

"What are you doing now?"

"I did some work on the garden as soon as I got here. Now I'm mowing the lawn. How are you making out?"

"Oh . . . fine. Okay."

"Well, thanks for calling. You take it easy now."

"Yes, Dad. I will."

Hearing him only increased the emptiness I felt. Next I called my mother at my grandmother's house, explaining what had happened in our session with Doug.

"I'm so glad it all turned out," she said, then hesitated for several long beats. "You know, Kathy, I had a part in this too."

"I know," I said softly.

"And I promise you that when I get home I'll sit down with Dad and we'll talk about this thing and get to the bottom of it. We'll try to understand why it happened."

I was glad for her admission of culpability and her pledge not to sweep it all under the rug. But they didn't alleviate my sense of desolation. Only sex could do that, as it always had, however momentarily, even if it was just with myself. All emotion, need, desire seemed to lead, for me, to a sexual act. It was my security, my affirmation of self, my consolation, however slight. I masturbated and fell quickly asleep.

The next day was better, lit by the usual California sun, which I bathed in for a few hours. I was able to read, write a little, take a walk exploring the area, and, that night, attend the Parents United meeting.

To hear a roomful of people discussing incest honestly, without inhibition, was stimulating and satisfying. Nevertheless, I found myself growing angry with some of the women, who seemed willing, even eager, to blame themselves for their husbands' actions. They implied it was their failure which led the men to turn sexually to their daughters. Even here the women seemed afraid of the men. And this infuriated me, perhaps because it hit too close to home. I remembered all the years I'd felt my mother choosing my father over me, unwilling to face the situation for fear of losing him, unwilling to rock the boat for my sake.

But despite this anger, my hurt at my father's early departure, the despair I'd felt listening to him revert to type after our session with Doug, the terrible fear and isolation of the last few days, I was able to gloss things over in swift and skillful fashion and, within days, declare myself virtually cured. Who said there was no such thing as a panacea? I'd found one. I'd looked into the past and disclosed what I'd seen. The whole family had talked about it. Dad and I had received counseling. Both he and Mother had apologized to me. Even Doug, the expert, said we didn't need further therapy. The air was cleared. It was over.

I wanted desperately to believe that, to believe that finally I was free. To facilitate that goal, I simply proclaimed a happy ending. It didn't last long. Almost immediately I found myself back at the beginning, with no end, happy or otherwise, in sight.

CHAPTER

14

"Dad and I love you very much. We'll be so glad when your life is better but life is that way, I guess."

—Mother

That fall I settled back into life in Chesterton and helped Polly prepare to leave on a publicity tour for her new book. She'd softened somewhat her earlier stand that we must live apart, sufficiently impressed by an agent's interest in my book to hang on a little longer, cautious about parting precipitously with an unindentured domestic. I, of course, as needy of her as ever, was willing to wait and see.

Soon after she'd gone, I returned to work on my book. Immediately, I was tossed back into a sea of old emotions, more powerful now than they'd ever been, rage the most potent of all.

How could I have dismissed it all so quickly? Shouldn't I be angry a little longer? After all, it had eaten up years of my life. Was it enough for my parents to say they were sorry? Did that constitute sufficient retribution?

Of course I'd felt better after going to California. Doug

had told me I would. You'll feel better now, he said; you'll feel a release. And because I was a good little girl, dutiful, obedient, I did as I was told. I felt better. I felt a release.

But it wasn't real. What was real was what I felt now. I wanted my father to die, a sudden elimination, heart attack perhaps, a brutal and fatal accident. I wanted him removed. And my mother. How could she stay under the same roof with him? How could she let him touch her? Worst of all, they didn't really know the extent of my pain. They thought I was okay now, purged of my terrible secret, accepting of their apologies, ready to get on with my life.

Maybe the book would *make* them see these things, make them know how I was suffering. I told them I was writing about them, about us. I waited for their panic.

"Good idea," my father mumbled. "You can get it all out of your system."

"I hope you'll make me look stronger than I was," my mother said quietly.

No satisfaction there. In fact, now I had a new resentment. They refused even to be intimidated.

The journal I kept reflected the increasing hopelessness I felt about my liaison with Polly, about myself, how powerless I felt to change any of it.

Polly says "I'm the center of the universe" just as Roger used to. What have I done to deserve another bastard in my life to use and abuse me?

Polly's right about me being a child, seeking a parent figure, a good parent, who will love and take care of me.

I like to be in [Polly's] power. I think I'm afraid to be in my own. After all, I never have been.

I can feel myself slipping away, no self forever. Romantic love blinds me, or is it emotional under-development? I know for sure if I stay with her I cannot grow, but how do I get away?

That was the same thing I'd said near the end of my marriage.

At Christmastime that year I met Angela in New York City and told her about the incest.

"When I was counseling with you," I said to her, "why didn't you ever ask if I'd slept with my father?"

"We only ask that of frigid wives or retarded girls," she answered.

I flinched at this affront.

"It may not be a bad relationship for these girls," she explained. "If it's taken away, what will they have?"

"Jesus Christ!" I roared. "They're human beings and you're letting a man use them. You have no right to do that."

My fury was gathering force and momentum. Sometimes it was energizing, impelling me into frenzied activity. Other times it acted like a sedative, making me fuzzy, nearly nonfunctional.

Letters from my mother often fueled my rage.

"I don't uderstand why all this happened in the first place," she wrote, "and I'm sure one could dig deeper and deeper to try and figure it out, but will that be of any satisfaction or will that just be another theory?"

I exploded when I read this. It confirmed my feeling that my parents felt they'd made amends—now they wanted to put the matter aside.

Even when Mother apologized in the next letter for those dismissive words, I felt only derision.

"Remember we both love you," she wrote, "and are very concerned always for you and would walk through hell and back for you and your kids."

Since when? I asked myself sarcastically.

Roger was exerting another sort of pressure on me. Feeling caught in a stranglehold by our disputed divorce settlement, he'd chosen to try to fight his way out of our complicated monetary entanglement by hiring a private detective to investigate my life. The results of that investigation in hand, Roger's attorney contacted mine to ask if he knew his client was a lesbian. I didn't deny it when my attorney confronted me. He asked if I'd be willing to part with one of my children. I told him absolutely not. They mustn't be separated.

The two issues raised here—lesbianism and the children—made clear to me the gist of Roger's thinking. He was prepared to threaten me with a custody battle, to use the children as hostages in our financial quarrel. If a battle were to be fought, he'd use my homosexuality against me.

My despondency grew. I felt in great danger. I had a sense of something awful about to happen. My fear literally paralyzed me. Some mornings I could barely force myself to get out of bed. Once up, it was difficult for me to perform the most mundane tasks: feeding the children, getting them off to school, doing housework, shopping. I was sinking rapidly. I needed help, and I finally found it in the person of Alice Friedland, a therapist in New York City. Starting in February, 1977, I flew back and forth between Chesterton and New York frequently, eager to see Alice whenever she could fit me in. I trusted her completely from the time of our first session, certain she wanted nothing from me but the fee for her services. I felt relieved and lucky to have her aid. At the same time, finally receiving proper help, I let go entirely and was nearly overwhelmed by my sickness. My repressive mechanisms no longer worked. Everything, every problem I had, every feeling I felt, surged into the foreground, creating pandemonium. I felt very close to total collapse.

Exploring my state with Alice, recognizing how precarious it was, I moved toward an agonizing but necessary decision. I gave Roger the children, reasoning that if I were ever to be of any use to them I must achieve some balance, some stability of my own, knowing I was not strong enough to fight Roger in court. I loved my children very much, but at that moment love was all I could give them and it didn't seem to be enough. They needed guidance, discipline, consistency. I was too disabled to provide these things for them. They needed someone who could put them first, make them a priority. I was disintegrating rapidly; if I didn't take care of myself, I'd go under. Roger loved the children too. My judgment was that he could provide them with a more stable environment than I could. It was that simple.

Its simplicity did not mitigate my despair. During a three-day blizzard that preceded Roger's coming to pick up the girls, the three of us were confined to the house, locked in with our anguish.

"Don't you want us?" Emily asked me as we sorted through her clothes, packing.

"Of course I do," I answered, sobbing even louder than she. "It's just that Daddy and I think it's best for you to be with him for a while."

Julia appeared unbothered in the daytime, but each night came to my room and begged to sleep with me, screaming, "You don't love me, you don't love me!"

I called Roger twice and pleaded with him not to come. But the matter was settled, so far as he was concerned. He'd pushed me to this point by threatening a suit; he wasn't going to lose his advantage.

After the children had gone, they haunted me. I saw their forms running down the street when I peered out the front window of the house, their faces shining through the school-bus windows. I heard their feet moving overhead, their voices whispering and giggling at the dinner table. I missed the unconditional love they offered so freely. I felt as though they'd died.

Ever since I'd decided to confront the incest, I'd known I was moving in the right direction, but nearly every step I took increased the pain. I believed my attempt to unravel the legacy of the past was positive, but seldom did anything *feel* good. My faith that the anguish was temporary, a necessary way station on the road to health, often faltered. I fantasized suicide; I wallowed in self-pity. My goal was often simply to get from one appointment with Alice to another. I tried to keep moving, putting one foot in front of the other, living life at its most rudimentary level. If I stopped, I felt, I'd die.

I wrote to my mother, telling her I'd given up the children and explaining why I thought it best. Extremely agitated by the news, she called me immediately.

"How are *you?*" she asked shakily.

"Not good," I replied. "It hurts."

I could hear her weeping. "It just seems to me," she said, her voice breaking, "that you're blaming Dad and me for all your problems."

"No, Mother, not all of them," I said. "I *am* blaming you for what happened to me when I was a child in your house."

"Dad's crushed, and he's angry, too."

"Well, that's just too bad," I sputtered childishly. "I'm sorry if he doesn't like what I'm doing, but at least I didn't fuck my kids!"

"He's become very despondent about this whole thing. He can't understand why you hate him so. He says Doug told him all he had to do was to say he was sorry."

"Jesus Christ, Mother!" I exploded in exasperation.

"Are you alone there?" she asked, quickly shifting gears.

I was, Polly having left the week before on a business trip. In fact, she was preparing to move out soon, bringing our relationship to a close. I didn't want to discuss this with my mother. I could barely face it myself. I knew Mother would happily pin the whole mess on Polly if she could.

"Yes," I answered curtly.

"Is Polly a help to you?"

"In a way," I said, still needing to whitewash Polly's image. After all, I'd chosen her. I was terribly embarrassed by how wrong I'd been.

"What's that supposed to mean?" she huffed.

"Mother, it's not her problem."

I closed the door on the subject of Polly, and Mother backed off.

"I just want you to know how much we love you," she said, her voice breaking again.

"I want to believe that," I said. "Please keep telling me."
Ellen supported my decision about the children.

"I think you've made very wise choices regarding yourself and the kids. Guilt shouldn't enter the picture at all.
Believe me, once you get yourself together you will all
benefit from this. Look at it like a rest."

My brother also endorsed it. "So now," he wrote, "you
must deal with the premature separation from your children and the time and energy once filled by them, difficult
for certain. Yet still, in relativity, not so bad. They are
bright, healthy, alive and whole, plus you will still have
much time with them and now an even greater chance for
you to grow and learn."

Letters from my mother continued to express her sense
of helplessness and confusion.

I'm sure if I'd talked to Doug in August we would
have sorted out things that I don't understand. I'm
still getting double messages because I'm in the middle as mother and wife (I'm not scolding, just trying
to understand it all). I try not to worry but it's hard
sometimes at night when I'm alone with my thoughts.
Dad and I have talked a lot and will talk some more
and also will see a counselor soon. He doesn't understand either himself or me or my concern to try and
understand at all. I pray that someday things will be
different.

I heard nothing from my father. He was vexed that I
didn't accept his apology to me in the session with Doug
as sufficient. When I wrote my mother asking if she
thought there was any history of incest on either side of
the family, he declared himself disgusted by my question,

saying, "My mother had nothing to do with it." I'd told Roger about the incest the day he came to pick up the children, requesting that he be present when my father visited the kids, that they not be allowed to go off with him alone. This demolished my father. He was now exposed before Roger. He was, he protested, being treated like a child molester. He decided I was "out to get" him.

The air of détente which had existed in the autumn was thoroughly destroyed by the spring. The family was at war. I, like a good general, sought a precise head count of my troops. Who was on my side? Who was on his? This was the only way I could see it. To offer me anything less than one hundred percent agreement with my views was to condone my father's behavior. But the rest of the family wasn't willing to obliterate Dad's place in their lives. My paranoia grew, fueled by what I saw as betrayal all about me.

Ellen, seeing a newly completed outline of my book, stopped writing to me. She said she was afraid I'd "use [the letters] against" her. When Dad attempted to talk to her about the incest, she said: "Oh, forget it. We don't need to talk about it. It's all in the past."

Mother's letters reverted to chatty epistles filled with the minutiae of day-to-day Middle American life. She signed them "Mom and Dad."

Andy also seemed to have adopted a very pacific tone.

"One thing I feel would be a step toward understanding each other more," he said in a letter, "is a time when you, Ellen, Mom, Dad, and I sit down *together* for the sole purpose of letting one another know how each of us feels and thinks. It doesn't seem like too much to ask for considering all the shit that's gone down over the years."

This felt like heresy to me. I invited Andy to visit me in

New York City, where I was now living. He'd suffered for years under Dad's repressive regime at home and then rebelled, refusing to play sports, going AWOL from the Army, rejecting conventional jobs, and living on small grants that underwrote music programs for young children in urban areas. Surely he'd line up on my side.

But when he arrived and we talked, I found him elusive and vague. He continually refused to give me what I wanted to hear: a blanket condemnation of Dad. Of course he condemned the incest, he said. But he saw Dad as more than just an incest offender. No, he didn't think I was crazy, any crazier than the rest of the family. Yes, he'd wondered about the book I was writing, wondered about my motives.

He never sided with me unconditionally on any issue we discussed. I had wanted Andy as an ally; I felt I'd found an adversary.

The only time I received the unqualified love and support I craved was during monthly visits to my children. They were delighted to see me, unstinting in their adoration, unquestioning in their acceptance of my love for them. The other side of the coin was that seeing them released feelings of guilt and powerlessness and sadness and reminded me how terribly lonely I was for them. Our partings were almost unbearable, Emily invariably begging to come along, saying she "couldn't make it without" me. It took me days to recover from these trips, each time climbing slowly out of the abyss, clinging to my belief that I'd made the right decision and to my faith that one day I'd be strong enough to have them back with me.

During my second visit to the children my parents arrived home from two months in Florida. I refused to see my father, fearing that he would turn me again into the child that he could manipulate, that he would rob me of the tiny pieces of adulthood I'd begun to accumulate. He called me at the motel where I was staying.

"You should see what you're doing to your mother," he said in his gruffest voice, Mother's weeping clearly audible in the background.

"No, Dad," I protested, "*you're* the cause of this, not me. And I won't discuss it with you. I will talk to Mother, though, when she's able to."

"You can't treat us like this," she wailed when she called me back. "Who do you think you are? We have to talk to each other."

I agreed to let her come to the motel. She stormed into my room, crying, wild-eyed.

"How can you just cut us off?" she asked. "And after all we've done for you?"

"I'm not cutting you off, Mother," I explained. "I can't see Dad right now. I have to think of myself first, to take care of myself, to do whatever will make me well. I hope you'll be able to understand that."

"Well, I don't know," she sputtered. "I just don't know, Kathy. I don't know what to do with this thing . . . how to begin to understand it . . . or get help with it. I just don't know."

"Jesus, Mother," I said with impatience, grabbing a phone book, quickly leafing through to find a heading labeled "Counselling," "there's a page of numbers you can call for help if you really want to, but I can't do it for you."

She took a number and called the next day for an appointment. This indicated to me that she was trying, that she wanted to understand what had happened to all of us.

Still, my paranoia whispered, is it enough? If she really had any sense of what this was all about, wouldn't she leave him?

I never told Andy that he'd let me down. In fact, despite my doubts, I turned to him more and more to relieve my sense of isolation. My need for a compatriot within the family was greater than my reservations about where his sympathies lay. To form an alliance with him, however, I had to extinguish those reservations. My reality-canceling apparatus made that easy.

"How fortunate I am to have you," I wrote to him, "to lean on emotionally and spiritually."

In my will I named him guardian of my children if anything were to happen to both me and Roger. I shared with him my sense of progress and failure, the ebb and flow of my feelings, the details of my life.

Late in the spring my mother and I had another long meeting. She had seen a counselor several times since I'd last seen her. He'd inquired about the lack of intercourse between my father and me. I suspected the counselor felt that if intercourse wasn't involved the incest was somehow invalid, didn't count. Mother also reported that Dad asked her if she could imagine how difficult it was for him to refrain from having intercourse with me. This seemed to me another instance of Dad asking to be rewarded for his restraint. Ellen felt sorry for Dad, Mother said. Andy felt angry about the whole thing and didn't want to discuss it anymore. She herself, Mother said, felt ambivalent, angry toward Dad, yet eager to understand him. By the end of our meeting I felt more suspicious, enraged, disappointed than ever. They were all snakes! Treacherous. Unreliable. Deceitful.

Clearly, my anger was getting worse, not better. My

thoughts ran to revenge, often of a violent sort. I wanted to be paid back for every damaging thing that had ever been done to me. I didn't want to be free of my past—not yet. I wanted to be compensated for it—by punishment of the guilty.

I felt that only Mother was making any attempt to see my point of view. And her efforts, as ever, seemed impossibly modest to me. Still, she was trying. I did believe that. When she suggested coming to visit for a week during the summer, I agreed.

We needed desperately to understand each other. I wanted to feel her love and support. She wanted to give them. Each of us, however, had her own terms. We struggled in our conversations together to bring these into some sort of harmony. The emotional currents running back and forth between us buffeted us both. We ended every day exhausted. The next morning we'd begin talking again.

In simplest terms, what I wanted to hear from her was that she was going to leave Dad because of what he'd done to me. I didn't really care that she was exploring her feelings, trying to understand the family—past and present—making an effort to resolve her conflicts, though I certainly gave lip service to these ideas. What I wanted to hear was that she despised the bastard and was getting out. And she couldn't tell me this.

She could say only how she hated herself for the past, for not seeing, how she pitied Dad and what he had to live with, how she had to make peace with the fact that her family was no longer intact, how Dad was an old man now, and very sad, how she didn't know what to do next, how she was trying to understand it all.

Each of us was firmly entrenched in her own groove, wanting to come closer together, finding it impossible. Our time together was like a summit meeting that failed to live up to its promise, each side unable to modify its position enough to suit the other. And a mutually satisfactory compromise now seemed further away than ever.

CHAPTER

15

*"Anytime one of our kids has a problem, it
affects Mother and I. We love you and want to
help you. Please remember that, won't you?"*
— *Dad*

Emily and Julia did not adjust well to living with Roger.
He and the woman he lived with, Karen Olsen, had a new
baby, and the girls felt he was favored, that they were
stepchildren, outsiders. The atmosphere in the house
seemed similar to the one that had existed during Roger's
and my marriage: mistrustful, tense, uncommunicative.
Emily was doing poorly in school, frequently bursting into
tears, saying she wished she were dead. Julia said she wished
Roger were dead—another way to resolve the same conflict. The end of each of my visits was terribly painful.
They begged me to stay or to take them with me. I had to
say no.

Back in New York, I'd still hear their voices, in my
mind, on the phone during the weekly call that Roger per-
mitted, through the cards they sent.

"To Mother," Emily wrote in one, "I love you as much

as a song and as much as a bird and as much as the earth so never leave me as long as I live because you are the one I love."

As I grew stronger and healthier during the spring and early summer, I became willing to face how unsuitable the present arrangement was for the children. During this time Roger had convinced himself that I was truly an unfit mother. He'd had time to mull over what I'd told him about the incest with my father, deciding it had left me damaged beyond repair, deciding it was responsible for the failure of our marriage.

"If you'd told me about it seventeen years ago," he said, displaying his deep resentment, "I wouldn't have married you."

"I wish I could have," I replied. "It wasn't possible for me then."

"I wouldn't have married you and ruined my life," he moaned.

"Two of us ruined our marriage, Roger," I pointed out, "not just me."

He'd also decided that my lesbianism could harm the children. He'd been taught to despise "dirty homosexuals," he told me. How could one of *them* be a good parent? And he'd taken it into his head that when the children came to visit me in New York in August I planned to kidnap them, not letting them return to Great Rapids.

I was still somewhat afraid of Roger; I didn't really want to fight him. I felt, however, that I had no choice. The children came first, and I was certain now that they belonged with me. I engaged a lawyer and filed suit. The children were temporarily put in custody of the court.

The early autumn of 1978 was filled with skirmishes between the lawyers. Bob McShane, my attorney, was a gentle, soft-spoken forty-year-old, an ordained minister as well as a member of the bar, a patient man, a believer in the healing power of love. Roger's lawyer, Carl Behnke, was rather Prussian—short, stocky, piercing eyes, crew-cut hair—but willing to be directed by his client, a pre-requisite of Roger's. Allen Kanzow, who represented the children, another short, squat German, was a Great Rapids native of some sixty-odd years, and wore a full beard which matched his gray hair.

It gradually became clear that Carl and Roger would argue that New York City was an unsuitable environment for children and that I, as a lesbian, incest victim, and patient in therapy, was an unsuitable mother. Bob and I intended to counter this by my own testimony and that of several expert witnesses.

All during the fall I traveled back and forth between New York and Great Rapids. My separations from the children became more and more traumatic. When I drove them from my motel to Roger's house, they often whimpered aloud. Sometimes they sobbed. Once I asked Mother to ride along with us, fearing I might break down myself.

Back in New York, I saw Alice frequently, venting my despair, my terrible remorse for what the girls were suffering, my sense of impending doom about the outcome of the trial. I felt that Roger didn't really want the children; he just didn't want me to have them. He was still the stern authority, punishing me for having withheld from him what he wanted, the continuation of our marriage.

"I sometimes feel like walking out of my life," I told Alice, "looking at it from afar."

Emily began sneaking phone calls to me when Roger and Karen were out.

"Daddy says we can't cry, it just makes things worse,"

she said, sounding quite desperate. "Mommy, when are you coming to get us?"

Julia had grown more and more withdrawn. She would no longer speak to me on the phone from Roger's house.

During one of my visits to Great Rapids I called Ellen to invite her to the motel for lunch. She couldn't make it, she said, but inquired as to how I was. Strained, I said, busy with legal matters, but okay.

"You know, Kathy," she said, "a time comes when a person just has to accept the blame for the past and get on with life."

"I suppose so," I replied, "if there's something to be blamed for. But I wasn't responsible for the incest, Ellen, if that's what you mean."

She was silent, and we hung up soon afterward. I was angry and hurt by her lack of support. I'd heard she and Bucky were spending quite a bit of time with Roger and Karen. That hurt me too.

When the children had gone to live with Roger the previous winter, I'd arranged for them to see a counselor, Betsy Fielding. Roger had agreed, so long as the counseling was limited to their making an adjustment to a new place and didn't get into what Roger called "all that shrink stuff." Betsy was a thirty-five-year-old redhead with an energetic, jovial manner, and the girls responded well to her, Emily sometimes referring to her as "the only friend I have." And they'd continued to see her all year.

In the middle of November, Betsy called me in New York.

"Can you come right away?" she asked. "Roger wants to negotiate."

This was what I'd been hoping for: a settlement out of court, an agreement between Roger and me about what was best for the girls, not an arrangement dictated by a judge.

"I think he wants out gracefully," Betsy said.

"She could be right," Alice agreed. "Roger doesn't like to lose."

In Great Rapids the three of us met for two straight days. It seemed clearer than ever that the children were a smokescreen, that Roger really wanted to hang on to me. I was a good mother, he agreed. He didn't really believe the incest or my lesbianism affected my capabilities as a parent. What the girls really needed was both of us, available to them anytime on short notice. It would be ideal if I were back in Great Rapids, living down the street from him. That was impossible, I told him, as impossible as it would be for him to relocate in New York. We couldn't reach a solution.

I decided to stay until the trial, holing up in my motel, reading or watching television, seeing no one, except for the children on weekends, the only time Roger allowed. I spent Thanksgiving Day alone, filled with self-pity, very depressed. When Bob hinted to me in a phone conversation that Ellen might be one of Roger's witnesses, my depression deepened.

Finally, I broke out of my isolation and called Mother, crying, telling her they planned to use the incest against me, planned perhaps to use Ellen too.

"Oh, honey, I'm so sorry." She began to cry also, then called out to Dad. "It's Kathy, Tom, and she's all alone. They're going to use the incest at the trial and maybe use Ellen and she's crying. . . ."

"What can we do?" Dad asked in the background. "Tell her we'll do anything to help. Tell her we'll go see Ellen."

I leaped at that suggestion, asking that they warn Ellen

she could be subpoenaed, warn her that Roger might try to use her at the trial.

Two days later Mother came to the motel to report on the meeting with Ellen.

Did she know, they'd asked, that she might have to testify? Yes, Ellen told them, she knew that was a possibility. Did she realize, Dad asked her, that this was a time for all of us to act together, as a family? She reacted violently to that, Mother said.

"You don't mean to tell me you're going to help her after what she's done?" Ellen roared.

"She hasn't done anything," Dad argued, "and I'm not going to let anyone take the blame for what I've done."

"God!" Ellen exploded. "Every time she shows up here there's trouble. She's going to ruin our lives . . . writing that book, telling people about incest. I don't even believe it happened."

"It happened, Ellen," Dad said quietly. "It happened."

"And you're really going to help her now?" She was still incredulous.

"Her kids need her," Mother said. "We're going to do whatever we have to do at the trial to see that she gets them back."

"They're better off with Roger," Ellen said.

"You gotta be kidding," Mother scoffed. "He's crazy sometimes."

"He's just different," Ellen maintained, "but he's okay."

"We'll be in court for as long as it takes," Dad said.

"Would you help me too, if it were me?" Ellen asked.

"Of course," Dad answered, "wouldn't we, Ma? We love you and we love Andy and Kathy, too, and we'd do anything to help any of you."

Mother's report did nothing to alleviate my uneasiness.

But I put it aside in the flurry of pretrial activities in the next week—briefings, hours and hours of psychological testing, interviews with the expert witnesses hired by Bob and by Allen.

The first day of the trial was December 19, 1978. As I entered the rotunda of Great Rapids's courthouse, the first person I saw was my father. I hadn't seen him or spoken to him in a year and a half.

He stood near the entrance to the courtroom, Mother beside him, smiling at me but a little wary, tears glistening in his eyes. I walked directly to him and reached up to kiss him on the cheek. He put an arm around my shoulder and hugged me gently. I walked into court, one parent on either side of me, feeling love and support from both of them simultaneously, without conflict, just as I'd always wanted to. If you wait long enough, I thought, all things come to pass.

When I sat down next to Bob he reiterated that Roger would call no expert witnesses.

"Then who will testify?" I asked.

"Your sister, for one," he said.

I was shocked, even though I'd feared this might happen.

"Was she subpoenaed?" I asked.

"No."

I felt sick to my stomach. I couldn't understand it. Did Ellen care for me so little? Or covet her position in Roger's good graces so much? Was she punishing me for old wounds, or simply trying to inflict new ones?

I was the first to testify. My hand shook as I raised it to be sworn in. I could feel the perspiration along my hairline, under my arms. Bob led me through an account of the events of the winter before, when I'd given the children to Roger, elicited my sense of how things had changed since then, questioned me about my life in New York, my theories of childrearing.

Roger followed me, stating his contentions that children cannot be effectively raised in apartments, that New York is a dirty, scary place, that I was unsuited to be a parent.

In the midst of his testimony there was noise at the back of the courtroom and I turned to see Ellen striding in with Karen, seating herself behind my parents, wearing a coat I'd given her years before. She stared straight ahead, her mouth drawn across her face in a tight line. I felt as rejected as I had on the playground decades ago when she'd refused to play with me. *Poor little Kathy.*

When we recessed for lunch, Ellen stood near the back of the courtroom, waiting for Roger.

"Shame, shame," Dad whispered at her as he passed by.

"Who are you to say that to me?" Her temper flared. She looked ready to hit him.

"Yes," Karen joined in, "you who live in a glass house."

"Come on now, Tom." Mother tugged at Dad's jacket. "Wait a minute, wait a minute."

As Ellen and Karen exited, Roger approached.

"Why aren't you up there telling all about what you did?" he asked Dad.

"I'll go up there anytime and tell them anything they want to know," Dad said.

"Let's see you do it." Roger's tone was scornful, provocative.

"You think you're so tough, black belt. If you want to settle this thing, do it like a man." He grabbed Roger's arm, preparing to lead him outside. Roger pulled away in one direction, Mother hauled Dad in the other, and a fight was averted.

The second day was reserved for the experts. Dr. Wil-

liams, hired by Allen, testified that homosexuals do not
raise homosexuals, heterosexuals do. He also said that
lesbians are often capable of more affection and caring in
a relationship than heterosexual women and often have
fewer problems. His opinion, he said, was that the children
should remain in their present environment, the more
traditional Midwest, but that custody should be with the
mother.

Dr. Evelyn Ellis, hired by Bob and me, testified that lesbianism was not a problem in raising children, nor would
it affect the children's sexuality. She also asserted that of
course children could grow up healthily in New York City.
She'd been born and raised in Brooklyn herself. She
recommended custody be with me.

That afternoon the judge met Emily and Julia, talking
with them alone, meeting afterward with Roger and me.

"I didn't ask them to choose between you," he told us.
"You can't do that to children. You have two very beautiful, bright kids. I'd hate to see them get hurt any more
than they already have been."

Betsy opened the third day, documenting the difficulties
both girls had had since living with Roger. He was a concerned and loving parent, she said, but somewhat re-
stricted and inhibited in his interaction with them. Both
girls had often expressed an urgent, even desperate, need
to be with me. Her observation of my relationship with
them showed it to be a spontaneous and spirited one,
characterized by sensitivity and responsiveness. She recommended I be the custodial parent.

Next Carl called the principal of the girls' school, who
asserted that they were both doing very well. Bob cast
doubt on this by presenting one of Emily's report cards
from Chesterton, which lauded her sensitivity, her rapid

adjustment, her independence, and one from Great Rapids, which indicated that she was troubled and that she missed her mother.

Then my father, subpoenaed by Carl and Roger, was called to the stand.

"Did the incest happen?" Carl asked.

"Yes, sir," Dad said firmly, "and I was totally responsible."

My eyes filled, but I continued to stare at my father, blurry now through the haze of tears. He'd given me, again, what I'd always wanted to hear. This time I felt he wouldn't retract it.

When he finished, Mother was called. I'd been afraid she might break down, but her voice was even, her manner calm. As she began to speak, I was the one who cried. Never had my sorrow felt deeper, sorrow for this woman who had been hurt as much as I had, perhaps even more, by Dad, Ellen, Roger, by me, and all she'd ever done was love each of us.

"Did you know about the incest?" Carl asked.

"I did not," she replied.

"Why not?" he continued.

"Who would suspect that was the trouble in her marriage?" she asked simply. "It never occurred to me."

"Did you know your daughter was a lesbian?"

"Yes."

"Who told you?"

"My daughter."

"What do you think about it?"

"I don't define my daughter nor other people by their sexuality."

Next, Ellen was called. Her body was shaking visibly; her voice cracked frequently during her testimony. She put forth her beliefs that the incest never happened, that I hated men, that she did not like gay people, that I would make my children lesbians, that it was ridiculous and weird for me to write a book about incest. She never looked at me while she testified; she never spoke to me in the courtroom. I felt no anger as I listened to her, only sadness for the distance between us, awe at the depth of her resentment, pity when people laughed at some of her more outlandish statements.

Allen, the girls' attorney, was first to sum up. He emphasized Roger's income, his position in the community, his obvious ability to provide his children with a comfortable physical environment, the fact that the children were settled here now.

"I recommend," he concluded, "that the children stay here with their father, and I honestly do think they are well placed here."

I put my head in my hands and sobbed. I heard Mother muttering behind me, calling Allen names. Betsy was crying softly, and I heard Bob urging me to take deep breaths.

He summed up next, eloquently presenting my case. Carl followed him. And then the judge began to speak.

He disposed of the issue of sex orientation.

"That has nothing to do with the ability to be a good parent," he said.

He put the incest in its proper place.

"It was an unfortunate family experience that happened a long time ago.

"But we are not here to talk about incest," he continued, "and we are not here to talk about sexuality. We are here to decide what is best for these two little girls. I am impressed with the character of Roger Brady and I am convinced he loves his children and can provide them with an excellent home."

The tension was intolerable. I lowered my head and took hold of Bob's hand.

"And I'm just as impressed with Ms. Brady's character," he went on, "especially with regard to her children. Children do need to be free to grow. They do need a full-time responsible adult around."

My heart was thumping loudly, and I squeezed Bob's hand tighter. Behind me, Mother was praying aloud.

"We are here to decide who is the better parent, and I have to say I believe Ms. Brady is and therefore I order that custody be given to her."

I looked up, a grin splitting my face, surrounded by the sounds of happy cheering and clapping, then embraces, congratulations from nearly everyone. My father's arms came around me from behind, holding me tightly, and I felt safe inside them. Mother was beside me then, pressing her cheek against mine, our tears running together. Looking over her shoulder, I saw Ellen's back passing through the courtroom door. She was lost to me now. It seemed our family always had a piece missing.

"I think the decision is best for the kids," I said to Roger, who crossed the aisle and took my hand.

"Yes," he said quietly, "I do too."

I started to pull back, angry words rising in my throat, questions I wanted to shriek at him. Then why did you fight? Why did you put all of us through this? Why did you insist on staging this show? I stopped myself, saying nothing, just gripping his hand, holding it between both of mine for a moment.

I had my children back. Nothing else really mattered.

CHAPTER

16

"The cloud that has hung over us always seems to have gone and from here comes a new and better time and growth for us all."

—*Mother*

So many times in my life I've thought I was starting over: when I married Roger, when I separated from him, when I met Angela, when I left Great Rapids to live with Polly, when I returned from the trip to California with Dad. And each time I counted on magic—a new place, a new person—to make everything different, not understanding that I'd be taking myself along, that I'd be the ingredient that would determine how things turned out. It baffled me that they always turned out the same.

I couldn't trust people or I trusted them too much. I didn't like being responsible for my life but I resented the authority I'd picked to run it. Reality gave me a terrible time; I preferred to see things as I wished they were. I didn't do well with intimacy, either; it demanded an authenticity that seemed beyond me. My self-esteem was abysmally low, my immaturity level high. I couldn't say no to anyone. I couldn't say yes to myself.

Now I'm beginning again, this time as an adult with two children of my own. Always before I have been the child, insisting on absolutes, demanding reparations. Well, no more. That luxury, and torment, is over. I know too much. Black and white are seldom the colors in this grown-up universe.

My father is neither the splendid golden-haired Marine with rosy cheeks and a shy sweetness in his smile whom I worshipped nor the brutish, despotic monster whom I despised. He is a flawed and unhappy man of many confusions and some strengths. He tyrannized me for ten years, holding fiercely to his narrow rationalizations, adamantly refusing to see the damage he was doing me. It took moral weakness of an extreme sort for him to exercise his destructive will so consistently for so long. But recently, and in public, he took responsibility for his violation of me, and that took extraordinary courage.

I still tend to see him at one or the other of these extremes, but I'm discovering that many parts of him exist in the gray area in between. We talk now. Sometimes my anger flares again; his wariness returns. We don't trust each other altogether. But we do talk.

I share Mother's feeling that I must accept that we Crosleys are a fragmented lot. The normal, wholesome, *united* family I so desperately sought doesn't seem to be in the cards. Ellen is absent now. But I don't count her out forever. I've seen what time can do. And at least those of us who are communicating are doing so in a more thorough, more valuable way than we ever have before.

I've learned a great deal by telling my story. I hope other

incest victims may experience a similar journey of discovery by reading it. If nothing else, I would wish them to hear in this tale the two things I needed most, but had to wait years, to hear: you are not alone and you are not to blame.